To Nancy
from

Voyage into Ireland

Roger Bennett
Dunmore 2022

BY THE SAME AUTHOR

Virgin Island Sketches
Caribbean Sketches
Notes on the Nude

Information on the author's life and work can be found at:
sculpturestudiodominica.blogspot.com

Voyage into Ireland

By Roger Burnett

First Published 2018 by
Studio Publications
Antrim
Commonwealth of Dominica
Email: antrimstudio@mail.com

ISBN: 9781729493939

In memory of
NORMA BURNETT
(1946 – 1981)
Devoted wife and mother

CONTENTS

Map	8
Preface	9
Introduction	10
Through Dublin	13
Grand Canal	23
Upper Shannon Navigation	51
Lower Shannon Navigation	98
River Barrow Navigation	118
River Nore Navigation	145
Waterford Estuary	155

8

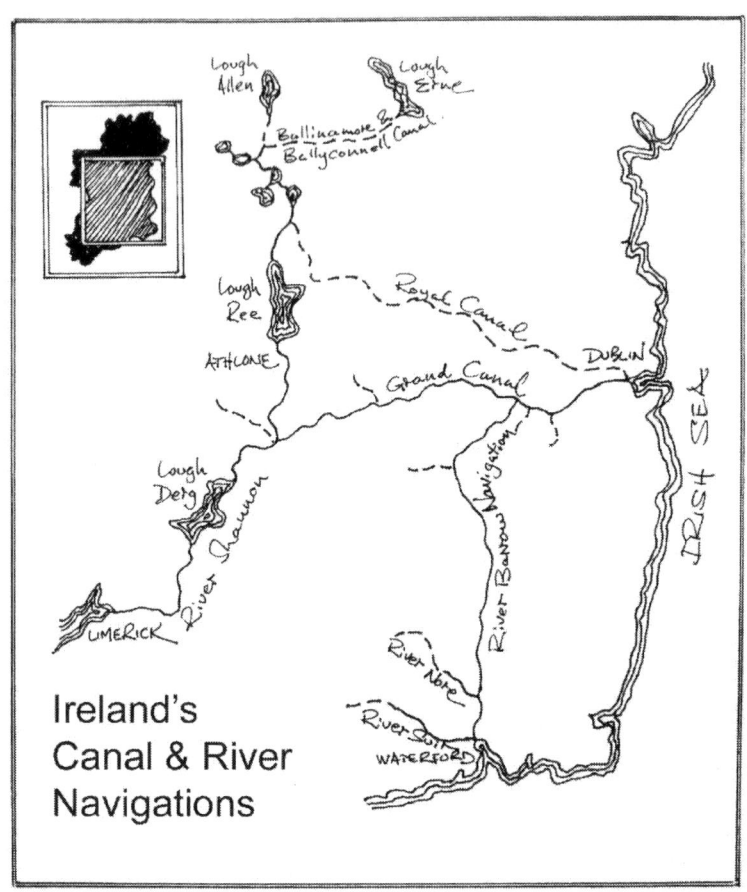

Ireland's
Canal & River
Navigations

PREFACE

Fifty years have passed since making the voyage that is the subject of this book. The manuscript that began as an up to the minute guide is now an historical document. Like the canals, it is a miracle that it has survived.

When my original publisher to put the book on hold due to financial restraints in the early 1970's, the typed manuscript took off on an amazing voyage of its own. It twice crossed the Atlantic aboard small sailing boats, survived storms at sea and two major hurricanes on land. For years it languished on a shelf in my studio, all but forgotten about.

Between making the voyage and retrieving the manuscript, there is a time lapse of half a century. During those intervening years the inland waterways of Ireland developed beyond belief. What was then abandoned is now restored and the navigations upon which we once sailed in solitude are now popular cruising grounds. I have resisted updating the text in memory of those earlier idyllic times.

Roger Burnett
Dominica
November 2018

INTRODUCTION

In Ireland they have a saying that the inevitable never happens but the unexpected often does.

Our every intention was to explore the canal route through France to the Mediterranean and, by way of a round-about return route, to include the canals that link to the Bay of Biscay and the inland waterways of Brittany. Preparations for that voyage were well underway when we learnt that the Dublin section of the Grand Canal was threatened with closure and that the River Barrow was rapidly becoming unnavigable.

A voyage into Ireland had always been on our agenda, but put off in the belief that the Irish waterways would be there for another year. But now that might not be so. The abandonment of the Royal Canal in the early 1960's had crippled Ireland's network of interconnecting navigations and just as certainly the closure of any portion of the Barrow or Grand Canal would mean the beginning of the end for all but the Shannon. So instead of sailing towards the sun we began planning a voyage to a land where rainfall is plentiful and frequent.

In his book *Green and Silver* L. T. C. Rolt describes a voyage through the inland waterways of Ireland in 1946. So little was then known about these waterways that his journey was undertaken in a spirit of discovery, as a venture into the unknown. With the exception of the River Shannon, Ireland's navigable canals and rivers were still virtually off the map in 1970. Ruth Delany's *The Canals of the South of Ireland*, an excellent and comprehensive history, had been written about them but little else. All the inland waterway maps stopped short at the Irish Sea and the Bartholomew quarter-inch and the Ordnance Survey half-inch sheets only scantily show the line of navigations. *The Inland waterways of Great Britain and Ireland* a reference book by L. A. Edwards, does include distance tables for Ireland's navigable waterways and by carefully measuring these off on the map we were able to put right some of the cartographer's omissions. The Irish Tourist Board sent us a pamphlet titled *Cruising on Inland Waterways* but it dismissed everything other than the Shannon in a single sentence.

From the Grand Canal Authorities we obtained a booklet titled *Pleasure Boating on the Grand Canal System*, an invaluable document in so far as it lists the names and addresses of all their lock-keepers. Ireland has a counterpart of Britain's Inland Waterways Association. But the Inland Waterways Association of Ireland has been so involved in the basic task of campaigning to save the navigations from abandonment that it has had little chance to produce anything in the way of information for visitors. There was a lot that we did not know and could not find out about, but such uncertainties can be the very making of adventure; lures rather than discouragements.

The converted Yorkshire Keel Barge that we lived aboard was too big and difficult to manage even on the large continental waterways when my crew totalled no more than Norma and our four year old daughter Diana. Before we could set off to explore Ireland's waterways we had to replace Jessica with a more suitable craft. Theoretically our barge could have all but made the voyage. Unlike England's network of predominantly narrow canals with locks only seven feet wide, the Irish waterways are broad and the smallest lock can pass boats very nearly fourteen feet beam by seventy feet long. But in Ireland, as in England, the bottom of the canal is often too close to the top and a deep drafted boat would frequently come aground. Weeds thrive and do their best to choke what is left of the channel. On the otherhand, the Shannon lakes can be cruel inland seas. Thus, the peculiarities of Ireland's waterways determined what our boat should be like.

It was late summer by the time we had found a buyer for our barge and well into autumn before we bought Jessica, a twenty-one foot long clinker built sloop with a beam of eight feet. She is comfortable and characterful and there is a functional look and feel about her. A temperamental 4 hp. two-stroke petrol engine pushes her along at a brisk walking pace but her sails are a more likable and reliable form of propulsion. The rig is simple and the mast is stepped in a tabernacle so that it can be easily lowered for canal travel. Beneath the cabin table is the center-board case and when the board is withdrawn, Jessica's draught is reduced from four feet to eighteen inches. We cannot stand upright in the cabin and even Diana has to duck when she goes to her bunk in the bows.

The early stage of planning a voyage is a delightful task. The real thing is a long way off and all things are imagined as being possible. But with only one month to go the limitations of reality begin creeping in and there is no end to the list of jobs still to do. This was the overwhelming state of affairs at the beginning of March, but by the end of the month and in a snow storm, we set sail from Littleport on the Cambridgeshire Fens. Ireland's balmy climate was a long way off both in time and distance. First, by way of 115 locks and 300 miles of canals and rivers, we had to sail across England. Not many people know that it is even possible. Our route took us down the River Ouse, across the Wash, along the Fossdyke and Witham Navigations, down the River Trent, through the heavy freight carrying Aire and Calder Navigations and then over the last surviving trans-Pennine waterway, the Leeds and Liverpool Canal. From the River Mersey we sailed around the Welsh coast to Holyhead and from there crossed the Irish Sea to Dublin.

THROUGH DUBLIN

Our landfall was Dun Loaghaire, a harbour on the south of Dublin Bay. While at anchor we lowered the mast for between Dun Loaghaire and the entrance to Dublin's River Liffey there are only three miles of open water and that we could do under engine alone. There was once a scheme last revived in the late nineteenth century, to link Dun Loaghaire to Dublin by ship canal. Had this come to fruition we could have started our voyage inland there and then. Before sailing Jessica through Dublin we spent a day in the city reconnoitering our route and obtaining a permit for the Grand Canal.

Downstream below the bridges, the River Liffey is busy with shipping. Up to the late 1950's smart steam barges passed up river to the Guinness Brewery to collect cargoes for ships in the Dublin Docks. We walked along the quay-side to where the Grand Canal connects with the river. At the entrance there are three locks of different sizes, and on a scaffold the words GRAND CANAL DOCK are sprawled in large letters. Alongside the small lock is a lock cottage and beyond the top gates a large deserted basin. We followed the basin around to its far corner where the canal connects. There was once a second basin but most of it has been filled in. The towpath had also disappeared and to get to the first canal lock we had to make a detour down cobbled back streets. From there on the Circular Line sets the bench-mark for canal townscapes.

The Circular Line was built in the 1790's as an extension to the main line of the Grand Canal. From the very beginning it was visualised as a scheme that would add beauty to the city and provide an amenity for the inhabitants. It is a green finger that stretches into the heart of Dublin, along which the best of man and the best of nature unite. As such it is worth more than all the park-ponds and municipal flower-beds put together. Big leafy trees shade a towpath trod through unclipped grass. Between their trunks are glimpses of fine Georgian houses. The channel is a narrow ribbon of crystal-clear water. There are mellow stone bridges and dripping lock chambers, the gates of which glisten with tar and on the balance beams sit a dozen dawdling Dubliners. On a hot summer's day the canal banks are teeming with sun-bathers and the full lock chambers are alive with swimmers. Had not commercial traffic, barges laden with barrels of porter, ceased in the early 1960's, what a multifunctional scene it would be. An Taisce (The National Trust for Ireland) regard the Circular Line as one of Dublin's most precious heritages. The City Authorities had other ideas. Up to a matter of months before our voyage it was their fervent ambition to channel sewage pipes along the canal bed and build a motorway alongside them.

That the Circular Line survives today in its navigable entirety is thanks to the Inland Waterways Association of Ireland, An Taisce, and similar groups. The fight for its survival and preservation lasted for the best part of the 1960's and represents a victory equal to the re-opening of the Stratford-on-Avon Canal. Yet, so far as I am aware, the story of this epic crusade has scarcely been told outside Ireland. As we walked its towpath that day our knowledge of the campaign was next to nothing. But fortunately, one evening early in our voyage, we were told the full story by someone who had been in the very thick of the fight.

Duncan Bain looks after the farming interests of a member of the Guinness family and, more important for posterity, cares very much about the future of Ireland's waterways. Duncan was chairman of the Dublin Branch of the I.W.A.I. during the Circular Line campaign. The following account has been compiled from press cuttings and notes, literally dispatches from the battle field, which he kindly loaned to me.

It was in 1961, soon after commercial traffic ceased to use the canal, that proposals were first made to use the route of the Circular Line for a new sewer and surface water drain that would serve the developing areas on the outskirts of the city. The City Engineer reported that it was the only economical solution and the only scheme that he could put forward with confidence. The canal would have to be abandoned as a waterway and become an underground culvert and sewer. There was a follow-up proposal to construct a six lane highway along the same route and had it not been for this the Corporation might have got away with their plan there and then. It was the fear that the drainage scheme would be the forerunner to a six-lane highway, rather than the loss of the canal, that caused the first public outcry, with the result that both schemes were shelved. The proposals gathered dust until the autumn of 1967 when they were put forward again, but this time the pill was sugar coated, though not very subtly. The Government sanctioned temporary closing of the canal on condition that the drains were laid in such a way that the canal would again be navigable when the work was completed. Ostensibly it seemed a fair solution but its viability was questionable and a disturbing aspect of the whole business was the failure of the authorities involved to make a full and frank public presentation of their plans. No tangible evidence had been produced to show that the alternative routes had been fully explored. There was an admitted absence of properly prepared costings: a "good idea" of the cost involved seemed a most unprofessional way of approaching an undertaking of such magnitude. Actually, the costings were in true canal tradition, for the history of inland navigations is riddled with wildly inaccurate estimates. From the engineering point of view many of the proposals were obviously impracticable. The rational was that the drains could be squeezed through the lock chambers and bridges without disturbing them too much. But the engineers were vague as to how an excavation width of at least 16ft and to the depth of 15ft could be accomplished through 14ft gauge locks and bridges without demolishing and rebuilding them; an unbelievably expensive procedure. The plans were also questionable in terms of aesthetics. It was by no means certain that it would ever be possible to restore the crucial balance between buildings, trees, grass banks and water. More likely the lock walls would be rebuilt with steel piling instead of the original masonry. Or yet again, once the pipes were down and the locks demolished, canal restoration might easily have given way to more pressing needs.

In their concern for the future of the Grand Canal, the Inland Waterways Association of Ireland had the support of over a hundred other organisations with a combined membership of

80,000. Together they formed a Canal Joint Committee and set up a fighting fund. One of the early actions that the I.W.A.I. took upon itself was to picket City Hall. Such methods have since tended to fall into disrepute but Duncan would still recommend it to anyone wishing to draw attention to a cause. It produced an immense manifestation of public support. A public meeting was attended by over 3,000 supporters and over 17,000 signatures were subscribed to a petition. With the help of an ad hoc body, The Friends of the Grand Canal in Advertising, thousands of car stickers were printed. These became a familiar sight, not only in Dublin, but throughout Ireland. A seminar was held, pamphlets were printed, legal opinions solicited, and meeting after meeting arranged with Government Departments. From the very beginning, the campaign was prevented from becoming a party political issue, as otherwise it would almost certainly have meant failure. The canal was frequently the main theme of newspaper letter columns. Critics of the campaign cited, with some justification, that even with the canal fully navigable most cruisers from Dublin bound for the Shannon go by road. From the amenity stand point the campaign might have aroused even more sympathy had the country been highly industrialised. Opponents to the canal argued that Ireland was teeming with green spaces and it did not matter if a few trees and a couple of grass banks disappeared in Dublin.

Negotiations went on through 1968. More signatures were added to the petition, voluntary working parties were organised to tidy-up the canal and businesses began put their canal frontages in order. The committee had worked to the utmost throughout the campaign and by the summer of 1969 it seemed that there was little else that could be done in defense of the waterway. For the first time there was some despondency at their ability to win through. But then, at the eleventh hour, came news of the canal's reprieve. The City Authorities had agreed to a new scheme whereby a separate tunnel would be built for the drains alongside the canal and the waterway and its environment would not be affected. To their eternal credit the campaigners had succeeded in diverting the huge steam-roller of bureaucracy away from the Grand Canal.

To get our canal permit we had to go to Pearse Street Railway Station. The Canal Offices are right alongside the platform: a paradoxical situation that came about in 1950 when the Grand Canal was amalgamated with Ireland's national transport authority Coras Iompair Eireann (C.I.E.). Until then, unlike most other navigations, the Company had remained independent. By the mid 1970's it is expected that the canal will be transferred to the administration of the Office of Public Works (colloquially: the Board of Works) the authority that maintains the Shannon Navigation. No doubt the Grand Canal and the Barrow Navigation will fare better when this comes about because C.I.E. seem to have lost what little interest they had in the canals.

We had been advised to tackle the Barrow Navigation early in our voyage, before the weeds took too strong a hold, but one of the weirs had been brought down by the winter floods. No promise could be made as to when the repairs would be completed because Ireland was in the grips of a cement strike. The lament of the weir seemed suspiciously like a reoccurrence of calamities that, since the decline of commercial traffic, have prevented all but a few boats from navigating the Barrow in its entirety. Our pass was made out for the journey from Dublin to the Shannon: 44 locks tolled at two shillings and three pence per lock. The toll went up a few pence later that year and has since gone decimal. We arranged to enter the sea lock on the tide that evening.

At times when it is most needed Jessica's engine can be depended upon to reach a new peak in unreliability. As with all two-stroke petrol engines the dividing line between running smoothly and not running at all is a very fine one. But by virtue of some other more fortunate quirk in its make-up it never totally lets us down. So although we motored across Dublin Bay with one finger continually prodding the carburetor float needle, the engine did not completely splutter to a stop until we were safely alongside the quay wall below the Grand Canal Dock.

Peter Moore has been look-keeper at the sea locks for twenty-two years and before that he worked on the Barrow Navigation. He told me that until this last decade there was busy commercial traffic; at times more cargoes than boats to carry them. There was a crew of four men to each boat: master, engineer, deck-hand and greaser. Between them they worked twenty-four hours a day, six days a week. When the working hours of the boatmen were reduced in 1946 the crew was cut down to three. They then took on an extra hand when they passed through the sea lock to help them load cargoes from alongside ships in the Liffey. Until canal horses were superseded by diesel engines, a steam tug named *Grand Canal* towed the barges to the ships. It was a regular thing for an empty boat to pass out through the sea lock at seven and be back in again with a cargo before nine. Peter and his assistant worked the locks while two clerks collected the tolls. For two years Peter was on the locks by himself, working the tides night and day, seven days a week, often going days without taking his boots off. Now it has gone to the other extreme. Occasionally a coaster comes into the dock through the big ship lock - one recently ploughed through the top gates and emptied the basin - or even more rarely, a yacht enters Shannon bound. Of the three parallel lock chambers only the ship lock and the barge lock are now workable. The middle one was for sailing ships and it has stood idle for fifty years. Beyond the locks, there was once a barge building yard and its dry docks are still shown on the Admiralty Chart for Dublin Bay. Peter Moore is a characteristic Irishman, immediately friendly and helpful and it is fitting that he should be the one to welcome boats to his land.

It had been arranged that the lock-keeper for the Circular Line would meet us at the first locks at eight the next morning. The weather forecast was excellent and the sun warmed the decks. The secret of sailing through Dublin unscathed is to do it during school hours so as to dodge the attention of children. It is the same when sailing through any large city, but in Ireland you have to be all the more quick off the mark because the school day is shorter. We had worked our way up three locks before the lock-keeper showed up. I worked the boat while Norma and every passing Dubliner heaved on the balance beams. In a similar manner we soon put the seven Circular Line Locks behind us. Alongside the top lock stands Portobello House, now a nursing home, but originally one of the hotels built for the canal passage boat service. The harbour from where the passengers set out has been filled in and is now a car park. After Portobello there is a two mile level before the junction with the main line of the canal.

Junk accumulates in any stretch of urban waterway and the canal through the outskirts of Dublin has its quota of car tyres, mattresses, bicycles and polythene bags. The Circular Line is kept relatively free of obstructions and along the Dublin section of the main line there has not been all that much heaped in. It is just that the clarity of the water makes it appear more than it really is. From looking over the bows, the channel beneath some of the bridges seemed completely blocked, but on prodding with a boat hook, obstructions that appeared to be only an inch or two below the surface were in fact four feet down.

Where the Circular Line joins the Main Line a branch canal leads to the multi-basined James's Street Harbour. It is choked with weeds to the extent that it is almost indistinguishable from the canal bank. In the days of commercial carrying James's Street Harbour was a centre of canal activities. Canal maintenance was based there, as was also the Guinness Brewery fleet. A good account of the workings of the harbour is given in *Portrait of the*

Grand Canal by Gerard D'Arcy.

The first seven locks on the main line come thick and fast and what little offensive development there is along the Grand Canal lies between them. The first lock is a double one, the equivalent of a staircase or riser lock in English canal terminology. One chamber leads directly into the next, the deep intermediate gates dually serving as top gates for the lower chamber and bottom gates for the upper. There are four double locks along the main line of the Grand Canal and three on the Barrow Navigation. Incidentally, a double lock in Ireland counts as one! All the lock-keepers turned out to help us at their respective locks, although one or two of them took some finding. Fortunately our Leeds and Liverpool Canal windlass was man-enough for the paddle mechanisms and therefore we could work independently when need be. What was occasionally lacking in the way of professional help was more than compensated for by willing onlookers. A hot summer's day, strikes, unemployment and truant guaranteed us a mixed and plentiful supply. And they did help, which is more than can often be said for onlookers of other lands. The same was true of the tinkers that camp alongside the seventh lock. It is an area reputed to be the worst for vandalism - one year the gates were burned down - but the only thing that we were showered with were questions about our journey. At each lock we simultaneously carried on a dozen conversations.

Beyond the eighth lock, and within an hour's walk from the center of Dublin, open countryside begins to make an appearance. We took our time up the remainder of the flight: the worst was over with. When in sight of the twelfth and last lock, and when we were least expecting it, we had our only mishap that day. Realising that our mooring would be to a grass bank, Norma began to search beneath the cockpit floor for the mooring pins, forgetting that the prop-shaft was turning and likely to catch hold of unsuspecting locks of hair. Fortunately the accident was not as bad as it might have been, but for the rest of the voyage Norma had a tender bald patch to remind her of it.

At the top lock there is a scattering of houses, a mill and the inevitable Bar. A dozen or so boats were moored along the canal, some belonging to a small hire fleet that is based there. How long I wondered can this last? Situated as it is alongside an amenity of growing importance, and within fifteen minutes by car the metropolis, the village is ripe for development. No doubt the next time I climb the canal from Dublin I will have to travel beyond a Twelfth Lock Marina before being reaching the back-of-beyond. As it was we drove our hard won moorings pins into the bank across from the Bar and jumped in for a swim. It was something that we had been promising ourselves all day.

THE GRAND CANAL

Two of the boats moored above the twelfth lock were converted Dutch barges and aboard one of them lived the laziest man in the world; at least that is the title by which he said I should to mention him by. He had the plum mooring right outside the Bar and it was impossible to pass that way without getting caught in conversation. At the time he was, as he put it, "raising a mast" and had that spar not been there on his deck for us to see we might have held an image of him patiently cultivating a likely tree.

We remained at that mooring for three days during which time I returned to Dublin to make some sketches and explore sections of the Royal Canal. The twelfth lock is within a mile of a bus route and the journey to Dublin was easily accomplished. It was not the busy commuter service that you might expect to find on the edge of a capital city. Even here the population is so sparse that there are no recognised bus stops. Instead you just stand and put your hand out anywhere along the road. I think the bus runs hourly, or it might be every other, but certainly for anyone not wishing to take their boat down into Dublin the Twelfth Lock is a good base from which to visit the city. Hire boat crews are not allowed to tackle the voyage in any case.

Getting across country to see the Royal Canal is a different matter as there are no buses. From the Twelfth Lock the Royal Canal is within walking distance, albeit a long walk, but instead I hitch-hiked. I have travelled many thousands of miles in this manner and it is an ideal way of getting to know a country. You meet people on their own terms and conversations range from pigs to politics. My first lift was in a rattling old wagon that carried "grass", the driver of which was determined that I should visit Wicklow rather than a canal he had not heard of. Two more lifts and I was at the town of Kilcock on the Royal Canal.

Legend has it the Royal Canal owes its origins to a retired shoemaker who after a quarrel threw up his seat on the Board of the Grand Canal and vowed to build a rival line that would carry all the traffic. It was an ill-fated scheme from the start. Work was begun in 1789 but the construction was a succession of difficulties and the canal was not opened throughout until 1817. The main line is longer and rises to a higher level than that of the Grand Canal and its route to the Shannon is over more difficult terrain. It never achieved the monopoly that its directors had hoped and the shoemaker died a broken man. The amazing thing is that it survived for as long as it did. Indeed, it was carrying commercial traffic into the 1950's and it was not abandoned until 1961. Had it been able to hold out for just a few more years its success story might have begun, for ironically the very things that had made it a failure in its commercial days would now have been points in its favour. It is decidedly the prettier line of the two. More important still, it connected to the Grand Canal (via the River Liffey in Dublin) and the Shannon, and this would have been the best pleasure cruising circuit imaginable.

At Kilcock there is a double lock where the road passes over the canal. It is one of the six such locks on the Royal Canal, all of which lie between there and Dublin. The locks could accommodate boats measuring 75ft. x 13ft. 4in. Thus boats built for the Royal Canal were longer than the locks on the Grand Canal. But as the Grand Canal Barges were built with a beam of 13 feet they could pass along the Royal Canal, although they only did so in exceptional circumstances. Once such occasion, when a breach in the Grand Canal cut off craft to the west of the summit, the stranded barges returned to Dublin by way of the River Shannon and Royal Canal. These slight differences in lock dimensions, ridiculous though they seem, are nothing when compared to the wildly differing gauges of the English canals. During the years of canal mania, when scores of projects were going on at the same time, each company had its own immediate needs in mind, rather than an eventual interconnecting network. The top land rack sluice mechanisms at Kilcock Lock were of a type that I had not seen before. They had not the usual cast iron upright but were mounted instead on a timber frame and I imagine that they are of a more ancient design. Although the lock gates had rotted beyond repair the masonry of the lock chamber was as good as the day it was built. This is often the case, for like the Victorian railway carriages, canals were built to last. Above and below the lock water levels were down and the channel was thick with weed. But the canal had not been completely drained, as it has been to the west of the summit.

The towpath was so overgrown that I had to walk instead along the main road that follows the canal for the three miles to Manooth. On the opposite bank runs the Dublin to Sligo railway line. The original railway company bought the canal so that it could construct its line alongside the navigation, for that was the best route. Afterwards, the railway company throttled the water-born trade so as to better their own interests. This is a typical sequence of events in the history of canals. The railway clings close to the canal right up to the summit level at Mullingar and a return ticket to there would enable anyone with little time or energy to see something of the waterway. Up to the coming of the railway it was possible to travel from Dublin to Mullingar by canal passenger boat. Hotels were built at Broad Stone Basin in Dublin and at Moyvally, the half-way point along the canal.

After a mile fields divide the road from the canal but I was able to get onto the towpath at each of the two locks along that stretch. At both locks a bridge spanned the chamber immediately below the bottom gates. Set into the masonry of the arch was a stone plaque inscribed with the name of the lock, the date 1795 and the words: R. Evans, Engineer. Both of the lock cottages were lived in. On the outskirts of Maynooth the road leaves the canal but as the towpath was clear I was able to follow it to Dukes Harbour, a large and deserted basin that once served the town. From the map I assumed that the next four miles of canal could hold no engineering works of special interest so I caught a bus to near where the navigation crosses over the River Rye.

Although the aqueduct is a work of considerable magnitude it is not immediately impressive, in fact I walked over it before realising that it was there. But perhaps that was because my eye was attracted to an unusual length-man's house on the far side. The two end walls of the house are semi-circular and the couple who live there told me that they believe it was built like that to break the wind. The house has been in their family for generations but to the best of their knowledge all of their predecessors worked for the railway, not the canal. This it seems likely, as when the railway was opened one step towards neglecting canal maintenance was to dispense with the services of the length-men. As a length-man's job is preventative bank maintenance it would not have been long before the effects were felt. The couple could remember the last laden barge that passed by their front door. It was owned by Leach of Killucan, the last bye-trader to operate along the canal.

I had hoped to reach as far as the narrow rock cutting near Clonsilla where the towpath is carried perilously along the bank high above the water, but it would have meant a round trip of eight miles along doubtfully passable towpath. Back on the road it did not take me long to get a lift, although the driver's motives for picking me up had me surprised. He was an insurance collector come sociologist, eager to meet different species of mankind. At that time the hippy cult had been followed by the "make love not war" flower-children and he hoped that I might be one of them!

That evening we filled our water containers at the village pump. Many parts of rural Ireland do not have mains water and the village pump is a familiar sight. More remote dwellings, farms and lock-keeper's cottages, depend on small springs or catching rain water from the roof. We never suffered any ill effects from pump water and the job of filling the containers was one of our favourite tasks. Each day every household has to go to draw drinking water and consequently the village pump is a natural meeting place. And how much better off the Irish are for this. They have none of the social problems that go hand in hand with twentieth century living in more developed countries. Lonely Heart and Darby and Joan Clubs are unknown. In the localities where mains water has been laid on I am told that the people regard it cautiously; they use it for flushing the toilet but not for making tea! For me the village pump was an excellent source of information and my only regret was that I had to go along with polythene containers that were awkward to fill. The next time I visit Ireland I shall take a galvanised bucket. One hire fleet operator based on the Grand Canal refuses to fill up the water tanks in the boats. He insists that the hirers go off with a bucket and get to know the Irish.

The next morning we cranked up the engine and went happily on our way. A heat-wave had firmly positioned itself over-head and all Ireland lay before us. Soon after the twelfth lock there is a rock cutting and beyond that the route is through rich pasture land. We passed cattle cooling off knee deep in the canal and a neat row of cottages, their front doors opening directly onto the towpath. Ahead of us a most curious craft was making steady progress in the same direction as ourselves. Its two man crew propelled it through the water by means of a peddle-driven paddle wheel. Their objective was the River Barrow. I would be interested to learn how they fared, for their craft would no doubt have tackled the weeds better than Jessica's propeller. Weeds are not a problem along the main line of the Grand Canal, they narrow the channel a little but that is all.

We arrived at the thirteenth lock just as the lock-keeper was leaving for his lunch. We told him to go ahead as we would willingly work the lock ourselves. He was reluctant to let us but we impressed upon him that we had worked through thousands of similar locks and after some deliberation he went on his way. Along most canals in England it is accepted that you work the locks yourself, whereas in Ireland it is the reverse. In Ireland the lock-keepers believe it essential to see all boats through for the following reasons: first, through an honest desire to help; second, because they think you will make a mess of things otherwise; and third, because they cannot imagine that you would want to do the job yourself. On difficult stretches, such as the climb out of Dublin, we welcomed a lock-keeper's help with open arms. But when the going is reasonably straight forward we are happier doing the job ourselves. We can then work at our own pace and there is none of the ridiculous business of pushing on past all the best moorings because the previous lock-keeper has telephoned the next to let him know you are coming. Admittedly this does not often happen in Ireland. There it is more often a case of slowing down to the other extreme, but I know of one navigation in England where they time you from one lock to the next and woe-betide you if you are a few minutes late. Moreover, there is a deep satisfaction to be had from working locks. If that pleasure is denied me, I'd sooner someone else was employed to steer the boat on the levels between and have done with it. The lock we had let ourselves in for was a double one and the deepest on the canal.

We moored that night to the grassy quay at Sallins, a small town that was once a busy canal port. Today it is dominated by a processed meat factory, but if you stand with your back to it, the rows of colour-washed houses must look the same as they always did. The directors of the Grand Canal once had a scheme for building an atmospheric railway - a Victorian venture in silent speed - along the banks of the canal, from Dublin to Sallins. Beyond the town the canal makes a sharp turn to the left, but the route originally proposed, and started upon, was to continue straight forward and through the Hill of Downings by means of a tunnel. The line that was eventually followed passes through the rim of the hill by means of a cutting, the earlier excavation now serve as a linier rubbish dump.

Within a few hundred yards of the bend is the junction with the Naas and Corbally Branch Canal. The next morning we poked our way along it and moored below the first lock. The canal was abandoned in 1961. It was the year that saw the end of commercial traffic and the closure of most of the Grand Canal branch lines. In the case of the canal to Nass this was particularly unfortunate because it is one of the most delightful stretches of waterway in the whole of Ireland. I walked bare-foot along the verge of the lane that runs besides it. The sun had only just begun to thread its way through the branches of the beech trees that line the banks and the grass under foot was soaked in dew. There are five evenly spaced locks in the two and a half miles between the junction and the town of Naas. The masonry of the lock chambers was in excellent condition and even the lock gates were not that bad to say that they had stood idle for a decade. I suspected that the broken balance beams and the occasional missing bottom gate plank were acts that had been done deliberately to put the closure into effect. Most of the levels still held water. Half way up the flight I found another curiously shaped canal house; this one being triangular in plan with one wall semi-circular. Naas Harbour is a large rectangular basin with warehouses along one side. To my eye they are the finest group of buildings in the town but the local authority had different ideas. Pinned to one of the doors was a notice declaring the warehouses a derelict site and warning the owners that they must "rectify it in such a manner that it will not become a derelict site". A recent chicken-wire fence surrounded the basin but as I squeezed through without difficulty it cannot be impenetrable to children. If I return to Naas in a decade's time and walk down Basin Street, I wonder what the prospect will be. Since our voyage a voluntary restoration project has got underway so perhaps boats will once again be moored in the harbour.

The canal that once linked Naas to Corbally is a different matter. Although it continues for five miles without a lock a main road has been made over it. The canal never did pass through, nor lead to, anywhere in particular. Corbally Harbour is a place in the wilds with only the remains of a warehouse and a basin to identify it. But that was not always the case. There are still some old people who remember when the canal was busy with barges bringing barley to the maltings at Athgarvan, a small town three miles from Corbally. But originally the Corbally Branch was conceived as the beginning of a more extensive plan. The construction of an extension was authorised in 1808. It was to have passed through Kilcullen, Baltinglass, Kiltegan,

Hacketstown and then on to Killabeg, a distance of 32 miles with 14 locks.

The canal was just wide enough below the bottom lock of the Naas Branch to turn Jessica around. That done, we wasted no time in covering the next mile to Leinster Aqueduct as we were looking forward to bathing in its trough while the sun was still hot. The aqueducts along Grand Canal make ideal swimming pools as they are usually deep and weed free. Leinster Aqueduct carries the canal over the dark brown waters of the Liffey; the same river that we had sailed upon in Dublin. The water in the trough was so clear that we could easily see right down to the bottom and the huge coping stones were pleasantly warm to sit on. We even managed to entice Diana to come in with us. This was quite something, for although she has lived most of her life afloat she is not very fond of making personal contact with water. In the old days swimming in the canal was frowned upon and carried a fine. One of the Grand Canal Company's standing orders read: "For any person or persons muddying the water by washing themselves or swimming in the Canal £1 2s 6d".

We moved on to the next lock but one to the summit before mooring for the night. This lock is unique on the Grand Canal network in that it has been constructed with a reservoir - like a shallow lock chamber - alongside it as a means of conserving water. On canals water is a precious commodity, especially near the summit level. In England such a device is known as a side-pound. When the lock is emptied, half the volume of water is run off into the side-pound and stored there until the lock is filled again. It is then emptied back into the lock chamber. Thus, only half the normal amount of water is used each time the lock is operated. The reason why it is important to conserve water at this lock is because its rise is unequal to the rise of the next lock above (8ft 4in as against 5ft 6in). In consequence a boat passing through the 17th lock draws a greater amount of water from the intervening level than what it discharges into it as it passes through the 18th lock. There is now a pump that makes up the difference and the side pond has not been used for a long time. It was so overgrown and silted and I might not have noticed it had not the lock-keeper pointed it out.

Above the lock a weed cutting gang was at work. A specially built boat, resembling a giant aquatic lawn mower, was being steered up and down the weedy margins of the canal. It thrashed away furiously and the weeds it mowed down were slowly carried by the current to where a boom had been placed across the canal. At that point a floating conveyer scooped them up and heaped them on the bank. We had just time to see this sequence before they knocked off for the day. When the noise from their machinery stopped the only sound to be heard was the gurgling of water at the top gates of the lock. It was a glorious evening and a perfect setting. Diana soon nodded off to sleep while Norma and I sat in the cockpit until after dark, wondering when, at some unknown time in the future, we would wish ourselves back there.

Although we knew our exact location that evening in canal terms, that being above lock number seventeen, it was difficult to relate this to a point on the map. I have found that even the British One-Inch Ordnance Survey maps are not at their most reliable when it comes to indicating the position of canal locks. The Irish Half-Inch Ordnance Survey Sheets, even after making allowances for their smaller scale are no better and to make them all the more difficult to follow, some sheets are badly printed. In this particular instance the road appeared to be at the wrong side of the canal and the bridge a mile away from where it actually was. Also, the paper that they are printed on is not very substantial. It is the same with the British Series now that the cloth mounted versions have been withdrawn. I wonder if the Director Generals of the respective Surveys have ever had to open out one of their maps with the wind blowing and the rain bucketing down. And where maps are most used, these conditions are frequently the norm.

At day break a mist hung over the water and we had reached the last lock to the summit before the sun penetrated through. The level was down a few inches, doubtless a result of the dry spell we had been having, but there was still ample water beneath Jessica's keel and if anything this length of canal seemed deeper than the rest. Indeed this may well have been so for many of the canal engineers built their summit levels to a greater depth to hold a reserve of water. We began to leave the lush farm lands behind and the next few miles were a foretaste of the wilder and remoter regions ahead. First our route was through a rough quarried region and then over an expanse of bog land. It is a landscape that cannot have changed since the days when the passenger boats plied along the canal, and ahead of us, just as the water travelers of the last century would have seen it, was the prominent outline of the canal hotel at Robertstown.

The hey-day of canal hotels was brief. In 1780, when the section of the Grand Canal from Dublin to Sallis was completed, the first passage boat was put into operation. Other services followed and by 1807 lavish hotels for the passengers had been built at Portobello, Sallins, Robertstown, Tullamore and Shannon Harbour. They were not a success. Faster fly boats and an improved system of coaching connections soon made them unnecessary and in 1813 they were advertised for letting. However, the number of passengers that patronised canal travel continued to steadily increase until the arrival of the railways towards the end of the first half of the 19th century. There was then a sharp decline and traffic ceased altogether in1852. Ruth Delany's book, *The Canals of the South of Ireland*, and her recently published *Grand Canal*, contain excellent accounts of the hotels, passengers, boats and boatmen. Additional material on the Robertstown Hotel can be found in *Canaliana*, the annual bulletin of the Robertstown Muintir na Tire (The Irish Community Movement).

Robertstown reverts to something like its old hustle and bustle for one fortnight in August when a Grand Canal Festa is held there. It is an event organised by the people of Robertstown to ensure that the canal continues to play a useful part in the life of the village and to raise funds for the restoration of the hotel. Already some of the more urgent work has been done by voluntary labour and the hotel figures prominently in the Festa program of events. There are lectures and exhibitions, and each evening eighteenth century candle-lit banquets are held in accordance to the old canal hotel menu. As we were navigating the Barrow during the Festa weeks I had to hitch-hike back to Robertstown to sample the activities.

It is planned that a permanent canal museum will one day be housed in the hotel, but restoration work will have to be well advanced before that can happen. At present the museum is a make-shift arrangement and items are borrowed from various sources for the Festa weeks. The quality of the exhibits was high. There were relics from the passage boats, old maps, photographs and models. But there were many gaps in the collection and almost no attempt had been made to label or explain. There is the potential for it to become the equivalent of the Waterway Museum at Stoke Bruerne on the Grand Union Canal in England. In the meantime editions of *Canaliana* are important contributions to the literature available on Ireland's inland waterways.

An article published in *Canaliana* had me worried as to what Robertstown might do in an attempt to sell itself during the Festa. Indeed, the very name Festa had me in doubts. The writer of the article had wistfully speculated: "large car parks, paved and scenic canal banks, souvenir shops and period lamp standards. In 1970 this impending doom had thankfully got no further than occasional strains of amplified music.

The summit level ends at Lowtown Lock, less than a mile from Robertstown. Just before the lock the Milltown Feeder enters the canal. The supply originates eight miles away at Seven Springs and the feeder was once navigable, and still is for the intrepid mariner - up to Milltown. The Seven Springs and the Grand Canal can claim some credit for the distinctive flavour of a pint of Guinness for the water which is used in the brewing is taken from the canal near the eighth lock in Dublin. The following report dates from 1787 and should reassure both canal enthusiasts and Guinness lovers a continual supply.

The amount of these springs measured in the driest season was 96 locks full in 24 hours, which added to the present supplies may be considered inexhaustible; but should the trade be so excessive as to require additions the Company can at the same place make a reservoir covering 340 acres, eight feet and a half deep, and containing upwards of 30, 000 locks full. These are resources which no other canal in the three Kingdoms can boast of, and will insure to the public permanency in the great advantages of inland navigation.

At Lowtown Lock the water is so amazingly clear that it is possible to see down to the bottom of the lock chamber and watch the gate paddles lifting. Beyond the lock is the junction with the Barrow Branch. Our revised plan was to return to the Barrow after we had sailed the Shannon in the hope that by then repairs to the damaged weir would be completed and the river made navigable again. On the main line there follows a seven mile level to the 20th lock, and then a nineteen mile level, the longest on the canal, to the Tullamore flight. These are the levels that pass through the heart of a vast area of bog-land.

The Great Bog of Allen is wild and desolate, but not completely devoid of interest or activity. Turf is one of Ireland's major sources of fuel, albeit that in its natural state bog is 95% water and its combustion properties nil. Traditionally the technique was to dig it up and stack it in the sun to dry. Today the process is basically the same but the Turf Development Board carry it out in a vast and mechanised way. The Board produces about three million tons of machined turf a year. Over two thirds of it is used in turf-burning power stations to produce electricity, while the bulk of the remainder is made into turf briquettes for domestic use. It is therefore the activities of the Turf Development Board that dominate the scene, from the weird and improvised machines that scrape at the bog, to the tall concrete cooling towers of the power stations.

But the turf industry has only a limited future. Within 25 years all the areas of workable bog will have been exhausted and an alternative use for the land will then have to found if the prosperity of its inhabitants is not to suffer. The Department of Agriculture is experimenting to see how the land can be reclaimed and to discover what crops can be economically grown on cut-away bog-land. Ted Barrett, owner of one of the boat yards along the canal, has suggested an altogether different solution for the bog-land in West Kildare. The scheme was put forward in the 1969 edition of *Canaliana*. It is based on the physical similarity between West Kildare's bog-land and England's Norfolk Broads, itself cut-away bog-land flooded by the rivers Bure and Yare. By flooding unproductive areas of cut-away bog-land adjoining the Grand Canal and its Branches a vast and varied cruising ground could be created. These new waterways could be made with relatevely little expenditure and they would bring to the area a greater share of Ireland's most profitable export business, tourism.

John Pender is lock-keeper at the 20th lock. He and his wife have lived at that remote spot since 1910. He told me of the brief revival in turf traffic during and after World War II. To alleviate a fuel crisis the Government commissioned the building of 29 temporary wooden horse-drawn barges and these they leased out to bye-traders who then carried turf to Dublin. Still to be seen along these levels are the weathered bollards, seemingly set in the middle of nowhere, that were once moorings for these vessels. Also to be occasionally seen are canal milestones, triangular in section and marked in Irish miles.

A fine hump-backed bridge carries the towpath of the main line over a short branch canal that leads to the town of Edenderry. The canal hereabouts has given more than its fair share of trouble over the years and it exemplifies the hazards involved in making a canal through regions of bog-land that are liable to subside. What was expected to be length of canal in a shallow cutting and cheap to construct, ended - after several years of unremitting labour and enormous expense - in the canal being carried along a high artificial embankment. Even before the canal was opened, and the water had been let in temporarily, a breach occurred on the embankment. A severe storm caused a second serious breach half a century later. This cost the Company almost £10,000 in repairs and necessitated the laying down of 3,700 feet of railroad so that goods could be trans-shipped. In January 1916 disaster again befell the by then impoverished Company when a third breach occurred. There are photographs of this in the Robertstown Canal Museum Collection. The banks had burst in exactly the same spot where the earlier breach had occurred and huge piles sunk at that time had been tossed about like match-sticks. This time there were conflicting opinions as to the cause. One theory was that it was due to an earth-tremor recorded in England at the time and believed to have also caused a land-slide in Wales. Repairs took three months to complete, and it was on this occasion that some of the stranded boats returned to Dublin via the Royal Canal.

We moored for the night near the junction and navigated the branch that leads to the town early the next day. A mist hung on either side of the embankment, obliterating all but the channel before us. But this dream-like atmosphere promptly turned into a nightmare as we approached the quay at Edenderry. All that I dread might one day happen to our canalscapes is epitomised there. The old hefty bollards have been sawn off short and replaced by dainty mooring pins that pulled out when we tied to them. The grass quayside, perfectly fitting if left alone, has been pitted with fussy flower beds and littered with bogus wrought-iron furniture. All is painted clinical white. The bank leading down to the road has been grubbed up and made into a rockery. A chain-link fence cordons it off and puts the original heavy stone steps out of bounds. The whole is surmounted by a WELCOME TO EDENDERRY sign. Whatever functional beauty the Edenderry waterfront might have had - and I suspect that it was once considerable - has now been destroyed, albeit with good intentions. But not everyone sees it the way I do. One recent account speaks of it in glowing terms and suggests that it should be repeated throughout the land.

The long level ends at Ballycommon Lock, the first of a flight of six that lead down to the town of Tullamore. Joseph Sales is the lock-keeper and he comes from a family that has been associated with the canal ever since the time it was built. It is the same with many of the lock-keepers in these islands. The generation that are now in old age have inherited a unique knowledge of the day to day working of the canals and are able to give information about a past which is far beyond their own life-span. The oral testimony of these people is one of the most exciting and valuable sources of historical material in the land and yet it is a field of research to which little attention has been given. And time is almost spent. In recent years the boardroom history of our canals has been fully documented but their social history and every day working has scarcely begun to be recorded. This great gap in our knowledge was brought home to me during our voyage into Ireland and through afterwards reading the books of George Ewart Evans on the relevance of the oral tradition in East Anglia. A tape recorder is an essential research tool, for a note book and the memory can only catch the salient points of a conversation and much wealth of vocabulary and illustration is missed. I regret that this awareness had not become evident to me earlier, for then I would have set out better prepared to collect the material that was there for the asking at each lock cottage.

When I asked Joseph Sales why the level above his lock was down a few inches he told me that it was the westerly wind that had blown the water to the other end of the long level. Had not this information been given to me with such obvious sincerity I might have suspected that my leg was being pulled, for the explanation seemed scarcely credible. However, it is recorded in the minutes of the Grand Canal Company that in 1839 a great storm caused the water to back up and overflow the level to such an extent that there was only 3 inches of water above the sill of the 32nd lock and boats were stranded for nine hours. Tom Murphy at the 19th lock can give oral testimony to this fact for his great grandfather was master of one of the boats stranded.

Joseph Sales was able to tell me something of the days when steam tugs towed barges along the long level. The building in which he keeps his pigs was once stables and accommodation for men waited between tows. I learnt more about the days of steam from a paper put before the Institute of Civil Engineers in 1866-7 and titled *On the Employment of Steam Power upon the Grand Canal, Ireland*. Extracts from the paper were published in the 1968 edition of *Canaliana*. One of the early efforts to introduce steam power on the Grand Canal was made in 1851. Three steam cargo carrying boats were built, one with single screw and two with double screw propulsion. Although they worked successfully the speculation was not remunerative because their capacity was reduced by the weight and space occupied by the machinery. The boats were subsequently employed in the deeper water of the Shannon Navigation. Later experiments were made in which a boat fitted with steam machinery dragged itself along by feeding on a chain laid in the bed of the canal. But this was a total failure and it was not until the early 1860's that two steam tugs were introduced along the long level with success. The tugs were built of iron, 60 ft. long by 7 ft. beam, and they hauled three boats laden with 40 tons of cargo at the rate of three miles an hour.

But perhaps the very first attempt to employ steam propulsion along the canals of Ireland, and certainly the most curious, was made in the early 1840's when a Mr. Robert Mallet adapted steam power and paddle wheels to one of the passenger boats. The object was to produce a boat capable of doing the journey from Dublin to Shannon Harbour in one day. For this, a speed of 10 miles an hour had to be achieved with a cargo of sixty passengers and their luggage. An unusually long and narrow canal boat had been patented that could be parted in two. When joined together its length was 120 feet, but when split and the two halves placed side by side, it could pass through the Grand Canal locks. Such a design offered the least resistance to the narrow waters of the canal. However, the boat was of such extremely narrow beam (5 feet 9 inches) and so flimsy in build (half-inch oak planking) that it was difficult to put adequate power in her and to give sufficient foothold for the machinery. For the boat Mr. Mallet designed high-pressure engines capable of being wrought up to 40 hp. with a boiler of the locomotive type, the total weight of which did not exceed 5 tons. Screw propulsion was at that time unknown. Paddle wheels were fitted, but these were limited in diameter by the height of the bridges and in width, by the narrowness of the locks. Trials were carried out and some curious facts observed. When the boat was put in motion the speed rapidly increased to 7½ mph. As the engine reached half power the speed further increased to nearly 9 mph, but no amount of extra power from the engine, nor different patterns of paddle wheels, could get it to go faster. At these speeds a wave was produced, the crest of which crossed the canal close in front of the boat. Had the boat been able to ride upon that wave, as did the horse-drawn fly boats and as do racing dinghies today, the laws of physics are such that a much faster speed could have been obtained. As it was, only when three picked and powerful horses were attached to the boat, while the engines were at work, could the speed exceed 9 mph.

Just above Ballycommon Lock is the junction of the Kilbeggan Branch. In 1961 this branch suffered the same fate as most of the others in that it was abandoned and subsequently drained. There is no reason why it should not eventually be reopened, for in the eight miles to Kilbeggan there are no looks.

Locks play a dominant role in canal travel and those along the Grand Canal have some peculiarities worth mentioning. First, the terminology is different in Ireland. The top gates are called breast gates and the bottom gates are called deep gates. The part of the sluice that actually covers the orifice is called the paddle (as on the English canals), but the rest of the raising mechanism is referred to as the rack. The sluices set in the masonry above the lock chamber are called land racks, whilst those in the gates are known as breast gate racks and deep gate racks. The windlass used to operate the racks is called a lock key and the section of canal between locks is known as a level. A Grand Canal lock key is considerably heftier and has more leverage than an English windlass, with the exception of the type used on the Leeds and Liverpool Canal. We took one of the latter along with us and it did the job admirably. The extra leverage is essential because it seems that no grease is ever applied to the mechanisms. Also, the gearing ratios and the size of paddle are the same as they were in the days of commercial traffic, for in Ireland they have not as yet begun to devise pleasure boat versions, as is the trend along the popular canals in England. The ratchets, that enable a rack to be left raised whilst the look fills, are invariably worn and ineffective. To overcome this, the unofficial but accepted technique is to carry suitably sized pebbles and gingerly wedge them in the gearing. It is a necessary ritual in Ireland to see that the lock gates correctly mitre together when they close. Failure to do this could lead to the gates bursting open and causing a serious accident. Some of the gates seem less substantial than those on the English canals and perhaps that is why this caution is peculiar to Ireland, for elsewhere it is taken for granted that the gates will line up. The footboards across the gates rest loose on their brackets and are held in position only by two chains. They are fitted this way to prevent the danger of a boat being caught beneath them as it rises in the lock, but they are potentially hazardous as they tip up if you stand on the ends that overhang the brackets. Other factors that can make lock operations difficult is the absence of landing places below the chambers and the scarcity of suitably placed bollards to tie to. A relic from the days of passenger traffic is the pole holes set in the masonry of the chambers so that the crew could protect the precious fly-boats from scratches.

Through the early morning mist we descended the locks to Tullamore and moored in the canal basin. Tullamore Harbour, as it is called, was recommended as a safe mooring in all the books we had read, but that was no longer true at the time of our voyage. The warehouses that once enclosed it had been demolished on one side and burnt out on the other. A hire boat firm had been established in those that remained intact, but this too seemed defunct. The young rascals that are an inevitable part of canals in towns soon gravitated towards our boat, mischievous rather than malicious, the Tom Sayers and

Huckleberry Finns of this generation. I heard one say to his mate that we wouldn't stay there long, and he was right. After doing some necessary heavy shopping we quickly covered the two miles and two locks to Ballycowan and revisited the town from there.

Without anxiety for the boat I could delve deeper into things. New headquarters for the Grand Canal maintenance staff are being established at Tullamore and at the time of our visit lock gates were being made there. The manager showed me these gates with some pride but I could not wholeheartedly share his enthusiasm. A traditionally constructed lock gate is one of the pleasing works of man, but the versions built today pale by comparison. Instead of being built up from skillfully shaped pieces of oak they are fabricated from standard steel girders. In this age, carpenters and balks of oak are few and far between, whereas welders and steel girders are ten to the dozen. However, in the case of canals economics and aesthetics are often compatible. Apart from being more pleasing to the eye and pleasanter to the touch, a traditionally built gate is mechanically and economically the better proposition of the two. Properly built and cared for a wood gate will last a hundred years. (I was told that by a man who had been building them for a life time). They will stand up to the knocks and bashing about that is inseparable from the canals, whereas a steel gate when bent is rendered useless. Also, their inherent buoyancy makes them easier to work. But even if the plight of hefty wood balance beams and tar soaked gates had to be argued on aesthetics alone they still to win through. The future role of our waterways is in the realm of recreation, and shoving against an impersonal girder is no more my idea of pleasure than sailing along a concrete ditch. However, the design of lock gates in Ireland is superior to those that I have seen in England. The steel balance beams are designed to give a relatively comfortable surface to push against and the gates are planked with wood rather than sheet metal.

Whereas it is only in recent years that steel lock gates began to supersede wooden ones in Ireland, the scarcity of native hardwoods led to the early adoption of steel barges. The Pomeroy, the oldest boat still afloat on the canal, is built of iron and dates from the 19th century. In 1925 the present type of steel barges were introduced and today no wood boats remain. In comparison to other canal and river craft in these islands, the lines of a Grand Canal barge are not particularly graceful. Nevertheless, they have the functional appeal that all working boats possess. They measure 61 feet long by 13 feet beam. A Bolinder diesel engine is housed in the stern and aft of it is fitted a ballast tank. The tank is filled when the boat is travelling unloaded in order to keep the propeller deep enough in the water. The first engine was fitted into one of the horse boats in 1911, thus making the Grand Canal Company the first carrying concern in these islands to use motor barges. Furthermore, a top secret method of boosting the injection of airplane engines during World War II had been in use on the Grand Canal since 1917!

Three barges were moored in Tullamore Harbour, each having served differently during the days of commercial carrying. This was indicated by the letters, M, B and E that suffixed the number on each boat. On the Grand Canal they use numbers rather than names.

The M boats (M for motor) were those owned and traded by the Grand Canal Company. The origins of the fleet date back to the 1840's when the Company obtained legal powers to act as carriers. Previously they had been restricted to toll taking.

The B boats were those belonging to the bye-traders and they were known as hack boats. Bye-traders were individuals, or small companies, who traded on the canal in their own boats. They paid tolls for passage through the locks and on the goods they carried. The bye-traders came into their own at the busy malt and sugar seasons when there was more traffic than could be handled solely by the Company's boats. At other times they would carry for their own firm, since most of them had some other business to provide cargoes for their barges. Occasionally the Grand Canal Company would charter barges from the bye-traders to help over a busy period, and at times the master of an M boat would hire the barge from the Company and ply as a bye-trader. The hack boats were an odd collection of varying shapes and dimensions. Their owners were the equivalent of the 'Number Ones' on the English canals.

The E boats were those belonging to the Company's engineering department. Today the maintenance fleet comprises of those boats that were the best of the bunch when commercial traffic ceased at the beginning of the 1960's. The rest were sold to private individuals for conversion. Having once converted a Yorkshire Keel barge for living and travelling aboard I was particularly interested in the conversions that had been made of the Grand Canal boats. About 30 such boats were sold by auction in 1960 and they went at bargain prices. But to convert a barge to any degree of professionalism is a mammoth and expensive task. Norma and I had worked fifteen hours a day, seven days a week, for one whole year to complete our conversion. It therefore did not surprise us to find many of those who had bought barges ten years ago are still on the job today.

We stayed two days at our mooring above Ballycowan Lock. Diana made friends with the children from the cottages nearby and the lady at the lock house baked us some soda bread. Many people in rural Ireland still bake their own bread and Norma took lessons. She learnt that no yeast goes into the making of soda bread, but beyond that the recipe was a handful this and a little of that. The result is so infinitely better than factory baked bread that it is a wonder how anyone who has once tasted the one can put up with the other. Another good food buy in Ireland is ice-cream. The surplus milk production ensures that a few pence will buy a generous serving.

The ruins of Ballycowan Castle are situated alongside the canal just below the lock. There has been a castle on this spot since the Middle Ages but the remains are largely those of a fortified house built in the seventeenth century. Had these ruins stood in a more developed land they would have doubtless been festooned with 'Danger Keep Out' notices, but as it was we could wander around freely and take a chance on it toppling down on the top of us.

The canal continues through pleasant country to the 30th and 31st locks. We tied up for a while along this stretch and set ourselves up beneath the shade of a tree for a long overdue hair cutting session and afterwards we jumped in for a swim. Beyond the locks the canal passes through another wild and remote region of bog-land. The only other craft we saw along the ten miles of this level were roughly built ferry punts, one to each isolated cottage. Beyond the next lock the scene became pleasanter, and decidedly so the time we reached the double look at Belmont.

As we approached Belmont Lock we could see that there was a great commotion and soon it became clear what had happened. A large vehicle had become stranded on the hump of the bridge that spans the lower chamber. All four wheels were inches off the ground and it took two tractors to pull it off. The bridge is as much a hindrance to navigation as it is to unsuspecting long wheel-base vehicles, for it is positioned such that it is difficult to get the lines of a small boat secured. Above the lock is a row of low whitewashed cottages and below a group of warehouses stand idle.

Three more miles and one more lock brought us to Shannon Harbour. The harbour never served any place in particular but it was an important trans-shipping terminal both for goods and, in the early days, passengers. This came about because the horses could not haul barges along the wide waters of the Shannon. Cargoes had to be trans-shipped into sailing boats and later, into steamers after they were introduced on the river in 1825. It is likely that from the early days of steamers there was a trend to take barges in tow for destinations on the Shannon, rather than trans-ship their cargoes. With the advent of the motor barge the harbour declined into little more than a toll collecting and fueling point. But the Grand Canal barges were not capable of safely tackling the lakes in rough weather. To overcome this, three large motor barges were placed on the river and from 1945 onwards cargoes were once again trans-shipped for their journey to the Shannon quays. At the time of L. T. C. Rolt's voyage the two locks leading down to the river, originally built larger to enable the early Shannon craft to enter the harbour, were being enlarged yet again to admit the bigger motor barges.

At the time of our voyage, Shannon Harbour was a scene of dereliction. To dodge the payment of rates the hotel has been gutted. Shafts of sunlight shine down through the three floors from the holes in the roof, illuminating a series of corridors, door arches and colour washed rooms. Cattle roamed in the basement and the steps leading to the main door were overgrown with weeds.. On the door someone had chalked: Bed and Breakfast 15 shillings! The warehouses are in a similar state. What were once houses for the harbour's hierarchy are in good repair and still lived in. The village consists of one street, along which there are three Bars. In the middle of the last century nearly 250 people lived there, but since the population has dwindled to a fraction of that figure. There is rumour that the harbor buildings will soon be demolished. It will be a sad day if this happens, for with them will go a page of history.

Industrial Archaeology is a term that was coined barely a decade ago. Although the title might sound forbidding, of all the branches of archaeology it has provoked the most enthusiasm and dedication amongst devotees. Basically its purpose is to salvage and restore, or at least record, the days of the industrial age before the last traces vanish. It is an exciting world of flywheels and pumps, coalmines and steam engines, for they are monuments to man's ingenuity no less than the pyramids. The need for industrial archaeology is urgent for much of our inheritance of old iron is inadvertently being destroyed. It is a race against the scrap-metal merchant and the bulldozer. There is pioneering spirit about the work; its techniques have not yet been perfected, its objects are far from being generally understood and it provides a field in which the non-specialist amateur can do valuable work. The challenge has captured the imagination of thousands, many of them members of recently formed societies. One such group is the Irish Society for Industrial Archaeology. Although it might not seem obvious to the casual observer, there is a wealth of material for the industrial archaeologist in Ireland. It includes the navigable waterways in general and sites such as Shannon Harbour in particular.

We spent two days rummaging among the remains of Shannon Harbour. Amongst the maze of yards and warehouses we discovered the remains of the canal office. The facade of this building, once embellished in the certainty of brisk trade and rising share prices, has now crumbled and the interior is deep in cattle dung. Nearby is the old wharf crane, a weighty mechanism of' groaning gearwheels. Beside it stands a bollard with grooves sculpted by thousands of mooring ropes.

Two dry docks and evidence of steam powered belt driven machinery testify that Shannon Harbour was once an important maintenance yard. The design of the dry dock gates along the

Grand Canal is unusual. Instead of being double and opening as a lock gate does, a single gate pivots along its bottom edge and is winched down into the water until it lays flat along the canal bed. Both docks are in excellent condition and still in use. There is the wreck of a barge in the harbour, the origins of which had me curious. It was longer and broader than the Grand Canal barges, and timber built with beautiful bluff bows and an overhanging curved stern that extended beyond the rudder stock. Just forward of the hold was a massive tabernacle where a mast had been stepped. From the interior joinery work it was obvious that the craft ended its days afloat as a house-boat. James Connolly, the lock-keeper at Shannon Harbour, was able to tell me its history. It was a Dutch barge, brought across the Shannon many years ago and converted into the finest yacht on the river.

Opposite to where the Grand Canal joins the Shannon is the entrance lock to the Ballinasloe Canal. Originally a bridge enabled the canal horses to cross the river at this point but it was soon superseded by a chain ferry. The remains of this ferry are still to be seen and James Connolly can remember it working about 30 years ago. They took the canal horse on the ferry and lashed the boat alongside. Sometimes, when there was fresh water on the Brosna (a tributary that flows into the channel below the locks) they would get two horses going at a gallop and then, when the tow was released, the barge would have enough way on her to drift the rest. The Ballinasloe Branch was used for the last time in 1959 and abandoned two years later. It has since been drained. From the map we could see that it traversed some 14 miles of flat, featureless country and there was no inducement to explore its tow-path. More tempting was the prospect of the next stage of our voyage.

THE UPPER SHANNON NAVIGATION

The Shannon is the longest river and by far the largest area of navigable inland waterway in these islands. It rises dramatically from a deep pool in the hills of Cavan and from there to the mouth of its estuary is a distance of 224 miles. Ten counties border onto the river's 800 miles of shoreline and its largest lakes, Lough Ree and Lough Derg, contain between them over 200 square miles of water. In the first 10 miles of its course the Shannon descends 240 feet, and then another 100 feet just above the tidal limit. Along the intervening 150 miles it falls only 60 feet. The River Shannon drains a one fifth of the whole island and, according to geologists, has been doing so for 30,000,000 years.

We passed through the last lock on the Grand Canal and turned into the Shannon's reed fringed waters. Just which way to sail was not immediately obvious, for at this point and elsewhere, the river is a maze of islands and openings. We travelled upstream to Shannonbridge. The bridge from which the village takes its name has 16 arches and all but one is as solid as the rock from which they were built. The exception is the old navigation span.

This has a Bailey Bridge slung over it; a makeshift arrangement that seems to be achieving permanence as the temporary often can. The contraption shakes and clatters each time a vehicle passes and guarantees no peace and quiet for anyone that might unsuspectingly moor to the quay below it.

Four miles north of Shannonbridge, on the east bank of the river, is the site of one of Ireland's foremost early monasteries. Clonmacnois was founded in 545 A.D. by the son of a chariot builder. As an ecclesiastical center it had only Armagh as a rival; as a center of Irish art and literature it had none. In its heyday Clonmacnois was more than just a monastery, it was a monastic city with domestic and industrial buildings. None of the workshops and dwellings has survived, and only fragments of the rest remain. These comprise of eight churches, two round towers, three high crosses, over 400 early gravestones, and two holy wells. It is not surprising that so much has disappeared for Clonmacnois has had more than its share of misfortunes. Between the years 122 and 1552 it was ravaged by fire thirteen times, plundered by the Vikings eight times, assailed by Irish enemies no less than twenty-seven times and by English foes six times. It was finally ransacked and reduced to a complete ruin by an English garrison stationed at Athlone.

Clonmacnois remained overgrown and neglected until 1955. In that year the Church of Ireland presented the site to the State, which previously had owned only the masonry of the ruins. Since then the treatment and maintenance of the monuments has considerably improved. However, a tragic blunder has been committed by allowing the cemetery to be extended without an investigation, for new graves are constantly being dug through archaeological deposits.

It was to a new jetty and neatly clipped grass that we landed. Diana played roly-poly down the hill of the castle next door while I attempted to evoke the tranquil spirit of learning with which the monastery did once abound. But for my money Shannon Harbour is worth a dozen Clonacnoises. It is just not my sort of history. I have not the ability to imagine a past if that past is presented to me wholly in terms of the hierarchy and aristocracy of an era. I would sooner see how and where the bourgeois baked their cakes, brewed their ale and tilled their fields. To my mind, this is how the teaching of history falls flat on its face. For my humble interest to be aroused you have to start with the tale of everyman in the decade before last, and not the other way about. Perhaps if the good work at Clonmacnois, and similar sites in Ireland and elsewhere, could be widened in scope to include an imaginative attempt to illustrate how they fitted into the pattern of commoner things, a new and better informed ancient monument brigade would be on the march.

One little bit of Clonmacnois that particularly caught my eye was a stone carved with a geometric design, the likeness of which can be found in the decorations of the narrow canal boats in England. The origin of the narrow boat decorations is a subject of much speculation. All kind of theories have been put forward - from Easter European influences to traits of Victoriana - but none of them, so far as I am aware, suggest that they might have originated from Ireland. Of Course the geometric similarity at Clonmacnois cannot alone prove any relationship. Every school boy that has ever doodled with a pair of compasses has produced the same pattern. But there are other links. The paintings of the castles for instance, evoke the landscape of Ireland. In some of the castle decorations round towers are depicted and these correspond with the monastic towers that are unique to Ireland. At the bow and stern of narrow boats there is a design that resembles a string of coloured diamonds, of which a similar pattern can be seen painted around the doorways of some Irish homes. The decorative roses are also occasionally found in Irish house decoration, particularly on gateways. They also decorate tinker's wagons. Perhaps the most important point to bear in mind is the fact that a deal of Irish labour was used in building the canals, and it is almost certain that some of them would in turn become boat people.

Our objective that day was Athlone. Twenty miles or more in one day is an ambitious rate of travel by canal standards, but one easily accomplished along the lock-free and diversion less stretches of the Shannon. The view in these regions is an interminable one of tall reeds with occasional glimpses of a vast rural hinterland beyond.

By early evening the lock below the town was in sight. Through the binoculars we could see that a number of boats had accumulated in the lock chamber and the bottom gates were being closed. We slackened off and prepared to tie to the staging below the lock. But Shannon lock-keepers have a keen eye for stragglers. More boats through at a time means less work for the lock-keeper. Regardless of the partially closed gates, we were motioned in. Our initial feeling of gratitude was quashed as we realized - but too late - that he had continued to close the gates until the gap was scarcely wider than Jessica's beam. To make matters worse, a top paddle that had been lifted, as is the technique at some locks on the river, so that the flow of water helps the gates to close. We caught the gates with a thump. Fortunately no damage was done but as soon as we were alongside I scuttled off up the ladder to give the lock-keeper a piece of my mind.

We had to pay 3s 5d for the doubtful pleasure of passing through Athlone lock. On the Shannon this fee is paid at each look and at each opening bridge, and it customary to round off the charge as a tip. This is the only fee levied on the river, and a very reasonable one considering that there are only five locks on the main line of the navigation above Killaloe and for most boats only one bridge that need be opened. But I begrudge paying tips that are expected as a matter of course, preferring to save my tips for instances that genuinely warrant them. At this lock I doggedly waited for my change.

At Athlone we met up with the Shannon's most recent invaders – fleets of hire-cruisers. The town's waterfront was jammed solid with them and there was not a vacant berth to be found. We searched further upstream, between the road and railway bridges, but if there did happen to be a foot of riverside not taken then it was a safe bet that there was a sewer outlet, shallows, or some other snag. Had we known better, we should have continued until eventually the hire boats petered out and anchored off some inaccessible reed fringed shore.
As it was we spent the night ignominiously moored in a marina. Such places are just not our cup of tea and we usually avoid them like the plague. This particular concern was still in the course of development, and although it held every prospect of evolving typical of its kind - it sported a sailor-hatted Mickey Mouse as its emblem - it had the virtue of few other boats and an absence of mooring fees for the odd night's stay.

On the opposite bank we could just make out the silted entrance to a canal that was part of an early scheme to make the Shannon navigable. The Shannon Navigation dates from 1697. In that year a petition came before the Irish parliament to make the river navigable from Limerick to county Leitrim. Nothing much was done about it until 1755 when work was commenced on both the upper Shannon and on the section between Limerick and Killaloe. The old canal at Athlone dates from that time. The present navigation works were completed in 1850. In the intervening years the navigation was in a notoriously imperfect state and impassable at times for boats drawing more than 2ft 6in. In contrast, the later works were carried out on a massive scale, with the locks between Killaloe and Battlebridge measuring 120ft by 30ft.

Early the next morning boats began to pass us heading in the direction of Lough Ree. Some of these we recognised as being amongst those moored in Athlone the previous evening. Seizing our chance we quickly cranked up the engine and made off towards the town to grab the vacated quay space.

Athlone is the largest town on the Shannon above Limarick. Because of its strategic position as the gateway to the lands of Connaught, Athlone has figured prominently in the history of Irish warfare. The heaviest and most devastating bombardment occurred in 1691 when the town was pounded by fifty cannon and eight mortars. These fired between them, 50 tons of powder, 600 bombs, 12,000 cannon balls, and many tons of stones. The old town grew up on the west bank of the river, in the shadow of the castle badly battered in the siege but now the greater portion of the town lies on the east bank. This shift took place over hundreds of years. To the casual observer there is now no difference in terms of centuries from one side to the other, but there is a very apparent difference in terms of a decade or so.

We moored to the east bank and saw that part of the town first. Once away from the quayside it was all recent shop frontages and we could have been anywhere. We followed a sign saying Cottage Industries, thinking of hand knit sweaters and hand thrown pots. Instead it turned out to be a collection of mass produced bric-a-brac and printed tea towels that had never seen the inside of a cottage. But once over the bridge and away from the bits we were supposed to see, we entered a part of the town that has been less disturbed by the second half of the 20th century. Perhaps its inhabitants would wish it to be, for on the face of it the neighbourhood on the east bank is decidedly the more prosperous of the two. Yet it can clearly be seen in the before and after example of Athlone, that the supermarket is won at the expense of the individual shop frontage, and modern pub architecture is won at the expense of the Select Bar.

The Grand Canal Company used to trade extensively on the Shannon and remains of their depots are to be found at riverside towns and villages. At Athlon the depot was situated above the lock on the west bank. The fabric of the wharf and warehouses remain, but the spirit of the place, the boats and cargoes and the men who worked them, has gone. Heavily disguised reminders of those days are the motor barges that were introduced on the river in the latter days of commercial carrying. These are the barges for which the locks at Shannon were enlarged to accommodate. Two of them, the St James and the St Patrick, have been converted into hotels and they ply from Athlone to Killaloe and Carrick. The third is a converted European canal barge.

The Post Office at Athlone is remarkable for its stamp machines. They look as if, in earlier days, they might have issued rarities destined for the pages of Stanley Gibbon's. We were frequent visitors to post offices. Our mail was sent care of them, and because that year the banks in Ireland went on strike from spring to autumn, funds to replenish the ship's purse reached us via the post office counter. But this arrangement was not without snags. We had miscalculated our date of arrival at Athlone and neither mail nor cash were waiting for us. But rather than hang around for our mail to catch up with us we resolved to sail on and explore Lough Ree. I could travel back overland afterwards. In the meantime we had enough food and fuel and there was nowhere to spend the money we hadn't got.

It was late afternoon before we got underway. Our objective was a narrow channel that links two loughs that join the main lake a few miles above the town. It appeared remote enough on the map, but as it was mentioned in a widely read guide to the

Shannon we had visions of half the hire boats on the river making for it. However, in the two days that we spent there we did not see another soul. Perhaps they had all got lost along the way, for that same guide, to our reckoning, contained 118 mistakes. It was a marvelous spot. The channel is hidden in the reeds of Lough Killinure and does not reveal itself until you are directly in line with it. Even then, at first glance, it does not appear to be navigable. The entrance was no wider than Jessica's beam but soon the channel broadens out a little and there is a grass bank into which we drove our mooring pins. Ahead of our mooring the reeds close in again until the channel finally opens into Lough Coosan. As the crow flies, we were only two miles from Athlone, yet the contrast between the hustle and bustle of the one and the solitude of the other is immense. The channel between the Loughs cannot be more than 50 yards from end to end, yet it has a feeling of distance about it, of penetration and exploration, which would take some unvaried stretches of the Shannon fifty miles to achieve.

The next morning we raised the mast, a task that became a regular procedure for each of the lakes. If we had known the Shannon better, or had a more reliable guide, we could have left the mast standing and sailed along many stretches of the river. There are no bridges or low electricity cables for miles on end. You can see a bridge easy enough and it registers, whereas electricity pylons sometimes hide behind trees and their web of wires can easily escape notice.

The day turned out to be warm and overcast and as there was not a breath of wind we had to use the engine to get underway. We first went around to Ballydeeran Bay. The Bay leads off from Lough Killinure by way of another reed fringed channel. Lough Killinure itself is split up into nooks and crannies and altogether this network of lakes at the bottom corner of Lough Ree is a much more exciting cruising ground than you would suspect from a casual glance at the map. Ballykeeran Bay is said to be poor holding ground but with no sign of wind we risked anchoring there and rowed ashore to the village. As we were still within a few miles of Athlone I hitch-hiked back to see our mail had arrived. Fortunately it had.

Coincidently the driver of my ride into town turned out to be the manager of a company that had printed one of the early guides to the Shannon: a book by the late Col. H. Rice titled *Thanks for the Memory*. It was published in 1952 and copies are now difficult to come by. My attempts to obtain a copy of the book through the inter-library loan scheme before we left England met with no success. But my printer friend was so full of enthusiasm for the book that I was determined to obtain a copy. Perhaps I had been led to expect too much, for when I finally managed to borrow a copy I found that for the most part it dwells in Celtic twilight and this you have to wade through to get the down to earthy business of sailing directions. But the book was compiled in the days when only a handful of boats sailed the river and it is unfair to compare it with publications that have appeared since holidays afloat on the Shannon have become popular.

Of more recent publications, *The Shannon Guide* has a lot to recommend it. The guide is sponsored by the drink, fuel, and tobacco companies and is therefore good value for money, especially if you don't contribute to the publication by smoking, drinking, or burning up petrol. The guide was in its second edition at the time of our voyage. It is aimed, with a Norfolk Broads type of approach, at those who hire boats on the river. It is easy to read and has lots of large clear charts that are sensibly printed on wet and wind-proof paper. A unique feature of the guide is that the charts show the reed line along the navigation. The reed line is often a lot different to the actual shore line. Unfortunately the guide has not been thoroughly researched. Most of the mistakes are minor ones and individually they do not matter, but collectively they do, for you to lose confidence in the rest. This is perhaps just as well for one or two of the mistakes could lead an unsuspecting boat into danger.

Holiday Cruising in Ireland by P. J. Ransom did not appear until after our voyage. To the author's credit, he has not allowed the Shannon to dominate the book at the expense of Ireland's other waterways, both North and South. A chapter is devoted to the river and that is adequate providing that you supplement it with maps and charts of a larger scale than those that supplement the text. The Irish Ordnance Survey half-inch to the mile maps are as vague with the Shannon as they are with the canals. If you write to their office at Phoenix Park, Dublin, it is possible to purchase remaining copies of the one inch to the mile maps that date from 1898. These are sold at a bargain price of 12½p each. They are printed on cloth and in colour. Moreover, the standard of cartography is very high. For areas where the colour version has been sold out the edition can still be obtained in black outline style. The size of the sheets is only 12 inches and therefore 10 sheets are needed to cover the river. In the case of Lough Ree and Lough Derg the Admiralty has re-published charts which originate from a 1837 survey. These offer the most detailed information for navigation. They have not been revised since the date of the original publication and therefore the present navigation markers are not shown but, other than that the lakes have not significantly changed.

A point to keep in mind, regardless from where you take your information, is that the depths of the river sections are constantly changing. Apart from the inevitable rise in level if there is heavy rainfall, the river is regulated to suit the Ardnacrusha hydro-electric power station and in a dry spell they may run the level down to keep up the supply. However, this seldom makes more than a foot or so difference. We first noticed this change of level as we approached Hare Island. It was almost three weeks since there had been any rain and the shores looked as if the tide was out.

Hare Island is one of the eight large islands on Lough Ree. It is situated just off the entrance to Lough Killinure and from a distance it appears to be deeply wooded. The island has a small harbour but through the binoculars we could make out a private sign and something to the effect of a ten shillings per day or night mooring fee. Duly forewarned we anchored some distance off and rowed ashore. As there appeared to be no one there we wondered who would have taken our money had we boldly sailed in. Perhaps they walk over from the house at the other end of the island. One could argue that private signs and a heritage of lakes and islands are incompatible, they are but it is difficult to think up practicable alternatives. Someone lives, farms and builds a quay there, and generally cultivates the balance which in essence is the attraction of the place. They have a right to preserve what they have created. Regrettably, many are unwilling to respect the countryside and moreover, to accept it on its own terms. This means more than simply closing gates and taking your rubbish home with you. It means approaching open spaces in the right frame of mind and to let the planners know that we don't want all that surrounds each piece of green bulldozing and concreting over so that you can drive right up to it. You must be prepared to get out and walk.

We wandered along a path leads into the lush meadow. There was a profusion of wild flowers and we regretted that we had not brought our little *Observer's Pocket Book*. In this day and age most of us are brought up in towns and cities and have no inherited knowledge of flora and fauna. Rather than knowing instinctively, we must look it up in a book. But that is better than not knowing at all. In the meadow stand the four walls of a little church. Rather than being dark, cold and forbidding, as are many churches - a tomb that is a long way from life as it was meant to be lived - a ruined church in a field is warmed by sunlight and smells of fresh air. It is man and God in close harmony.

That evening we went back to our mooring along the narrow channel that leads to Lough Coosan. The long spell of settled weather had burnt itself out and there was every indication of the calm before a storm. We listened to the shipping forecast and that confirmed that we best get clear of Lough Ree the next day.

It seemed strange to be listening to the shipping forecast while tied to a grassy bank in the middle of Ireland, with a couple of cows grazing nearby. But Sea Area Shannon is equally as relevant there as it is a hundred miles out in the Atlantic. To state realistically what is involved in sailing the Shannon lakes, I cannot do better than to quote what L. T. C. Rolt wrote on the subject in *Green and Silver*. Remember, the book was based on a journey made in 1946 and therefore the following is something of a prophecy come true.

> *No navigator, however experienced he may be, can afford to take too many chances on Lough Derg. The very narrowness of the lake adds to the hazard since it affords little sea room. Consequently, in the event of engine failure or other difficulty, the unfortunate navigator invariably finds himself caught on a lee shore. I emphasize these points in case the Shannon Development Association, in their laudable campaign to popularize the river, should convey the erroneous impression that cruising on the Irish Shannon is as safe and simple as navigating the English Thames. There should assuredly be more traffic on the river, and I am certain that there would be if the cruising facilities which the Shannon offers were more widely known to boat owners in this country. But to encourage those without any previous experience to hire craft and take them out*

on the lakes would be folly.

This cautionary advice is not sufficiently taken on board by those who hire boats on the river and, understandably, there is reluctance on the part of hire-boat operators to push the point. It is full breasted blonds lounging on sun-decks that sell holidays afloat and not the possibility of gale-force winds and a rocky lee shore. While I have no desire to dramatise, it would be wrong to pretend that the dangers do not exist. The Shannon lakes in general, and Lough Ree and Lough Derg in particular, are large areas of water in which the wind can whip up a formidable sea. The resulting waves, though not large, are more confused than they would be in the open sea. However, with a careful eye on the weather and an ear to the forecasts dangerous conditions can usually be avoided. But when there is only a one week holiday boat hirers are unwilling to waste a moment waiting for the weather. It is then that the risks are taken. Squalls can blow in from the Atlantic with little warning. Even then, if the situation is quickly sized up, it should be possible to put up a good distance from a lee shore and seek shelter. To do so is a basic act of seamanship. But even the most basic acts of seamanship demand something more than the carefree holiday mood with which so many approach the river.

On the positive side, the hire boats on the Shannon rank amongst the finest in Europe. It is from this angle that the hire firms have done most to tackle the Shannon's angrier moods. The Irish Hire Boat Operators have laid down a code of exacting standards that their craft must adhere to. This ensures that they are sea-worthy in design, sensibly fitted out and well equipped. But a compass is no help to someone who doesn't know how to use it, and flares are no help if there's no one competent enough to go to the rescue.

There are basically three things that could be done to reduce the risks of the inexperienced coming to grief on the Shannon.

First, the hire firms should make it clear in their brochures that the Shannon is not all plain sailing. From a cross-section of brochures I only found one that mentions that the larger lakes can be rough in bad weather, and then goes on to suggest that those who prefer a less testing cruise should restrict themselves to the stretches of the Shannon above Lough Ree. This company was based within that safe cruising area, whereas any firm below Lough Ree would not be able to make the same suggestion. Admittedly, hirers must state previous experience at the time of booking and in small print companies reserve the right to restrict the cruising range in the interest of safety. However, the practical application of these Conditions of Hire is doubtful. With the right approach it should be possible to "sell" a Shannon holiday in the spirit of challenge and mild adventure. I believe that there is an underlying need for this. It has resulted in an enormous increase of interest in inland waterways in recent years. In particular it comes from those in middle age and those with a young family. They are unwilling to accept the limitations that have previously been attached to such circumstances. An emphasis on exploring rather than holidaying on the Shannon encourages a different frame of mind, one that beforehand would look upon acquiring the necessary knowledge and skills as a fundamental part of the experience.

Secondly, a lot could be done is to improve the navigational aids on the Shannon. As I said earlier, the principal guide to the river cannot be depended upon, but beyond that the scheme of the buoys and markers needs to be revised. Very often there is not a distinction in shape, as there is at sea, between port and starboard buoys. There should be, particularly as the red paint used on the port buoys fades to a light pink and is then difficult to distinguish from a distance. But more important, there is no means of identifying, either by number or by name, one marker or buoy from another. This is essential to the navigator so that he can confirm his position, not only on the lakes, but also along many stretches of featureless river.

Thirdly, on Lough Ree and Lough Derg there should be some form of coastguard and rescue service. Around our coasts these services are the established norm, yet on lakes which are veritable inland seas, there is nothing at all. Essentially, relatively little is involved. Inshore rescue crafts should be based on both lakes and crewed by volunteers. Both lakes need two coastguard stations that are at least manned during the hours of daylight during the busy hire cruising season. The service could help to solve many of the problems that hire cruising on these two lakes present. It could give a visual indication when conditions are too rough for a lake crossing to be attempted (supplemented with a telephone weather report) and also serve to report a boat that is being handled irresponsibly. Perhaps then their task of alerting the rescue craft might never be necessary.

As we did not want to be weather-bound on Lough Ree we set sail early the next morning. What little wind there was soon died away and we again had to resort to using the engine. But with the whole day before us, and a flat calm, the throttle only needed to be set at tick-over. We had planned a course that would enable us to see something of each of the islands on the way.

Our first stop was at Inchmore, the largest of the islands. It is roughly circular in shape and about a mile across. The map indicated that there was once a settlement on the island, including a school, and we were curious to know what remained of it. We anchored and rowed towards the small jetty, but as it became obvious that someone was living and working close by we did not intrude any further. This seemed to be the pattern on most of the islands. Whereas we had supposed that they were no longer inhabited it seems that they may be well on their way to becoming desirable places of residence. On Ichturk, an island just off Inchmore, there is a recent bungalow.

The same was true of Inchbofin, a long narrow island situated at the entrance to Derry Bay. At the southern end of the island a house looks over the lake. But as our interest lay in a monastery at the northern end of the island that is listed as a National Monument we assumed that visiting was in order. We rowed ashore and landed at a small bay to the south of where the ruins were shown on the map. Had we have gone on a little further we would have come to a jetty that has been built to enable access, whereas we waded ashore and picked our way through nettles before we came to the first of the churches. It was in the same state as the one on Hare Island, but within the walls was a chancel arch, simple and profound. There was evidence of recent activity by the Office of Public Works, the department with responsibility for Ireland's monuments. The jetty was one innovation and a locked gate on the church was another. Also, the undergrowth and ivy had been sprayed with chemicals. We followed a path that led away from the church thinking that we had seen all. But we soon came across the more extensive remains of the actual monastery. We enjoyed picking over these ruins for they conveyed a sense of discovery. They were at one with their surroundings and each person that approaches from that roughly trod path has the impression of being the first to set eyes on them. There is just the right degree of preservation and presentation. As an historical site it has the advantage of being a little remote and therefore reserved to devotees, rather than guided tours.

From Inchbofin we sailed past Nut Island and King's Island and the scattering of small islands that lie about them. We were curious about the origin of their names. Long Island and Sand Island can easily be surmised, but what about Red Island, Horse Island and Girl's Island? Astern the distant southern shores of the lake were a delicate grey blue. Sometimes film companies use the lakes for shooting sea scenes. One of their props, an exact replica of a Viking Long Ship, was anchored in the reeds above Athlone. We were told that the film gave the illusion of a whole fleet: the exact replica in the foreground and a flotilla of cardboard cut-outs following astern.

Blackbrink Bay is situated on the west shore of the lake and from there a canal leads to the small town of Leecarrow. The canal has been restored in recent years and although the level of the lake was low when we nosed our way in, there was still ample water beneath Jessica's keel. After a mile the canal terminates at a small harbour. The only thing that spoils an otherwise commendable scheme to provide shelter and mooring facilities, is the chicken wire fence that has been erected around the harbour. This economy "stop children falling in kit" has made its appearance throughout the inland waterways of these islands. The barriers are usually erected by Local Authorities to quieten complaining mums. But they are not effective. No fence, or at least nothing short of the prison camp variety, can physically stop a determined nine year old, all it can do is act as a visual warning to their senses. Under that age it is surely up to the parents to look after them. All that is needed is a low wall to break a child's gallop should it for a split second break away. A low wall can be a visually attractive and equally do the job of cautioning older children.

We walked into Leecarrow and bought ice-cream at the general store. Ice-cream is Ireland's best food buy, both in price and quality. An ice-cream sandwich is a good guide to the generosity of the shopkeeper. The portions are cut from a family-size block, so there is no hard and fast rule as to how much you will get for your money. In this case they were so large that in return Norma bought a bag full of shopping.

We got back to the boat just in time to hear the afternoon shipping forecast. Although Lough Ree was still as calm as the proverbial duck pond, gale force winds were predicted. We could have happily spent the rest of the day at Leecarrow but not to be marooned there indefinitely. To be on the safe side we decided to continue our journey while the calm lasted and visit islands along the way.

We anchored off Quaker Island. There is landing place on the east shore, but before setting off to explore we jumped overboard for a swim. The solitude of the Shannon allows this to be done without any more thought than just stripping naked and jumping in. On rowing ashore three cows chased by three men landed on the beach as we did. The pasture on the island is so rich that cattle are ferried out to graze and that afternoon some were being rounded up to be taken back to the mainland. Getting the cattle into a small open boat is not an easy task. The resulting struggle was excellent photographic material and I worked as determinedly as the men that shoved and heaved each cow aboard. The last one was the most obstinate of all and after half an hour they were no nearer than when they had started. By then time was getting late and were anxious to be on our way. Reluctantly I interrupted their struggle to ask if they would like copies of the photographs sending on, and if so to what address. As soon as they broke off the cow stepped aboard the boat of its own accord!

Quaker Island was once another of the Lough Ree monastic settlements. One of its churches is said to be the smallest in Ireland with interior measures of 8 feet by 7 feet. The Quaker's House from which the island gets its name (or rather its present name, for originally it was known as Incholeraun) dates from 1837. To my eye, more memorable than the remains was the view from the ruins of a small farm house. In these days architects seem committed to incorporating picture windows in every house, even though the view seldom amounts to more than an identical picture window of the house opposite. But here it was the other way about. The window was no more than a couple of feet square, yet the view looked out across the lake to the rich meadows of the mainland and the mountains beyond.

By the time we got back the boat it was early evening. A slight breeze had sprung and we were able to set the sails. The main course for the northern part of the lake lies between a string of islands and the east shore, and then diverts towards the west shore after the last of them. The wind was steadily strengthening but we were soon in sheltered water and anchored in a reed fringed inlet below the bridge at Lanesborough. Later that night, and during the days that followed, it blew a gale.

Just beyond the bridge at Lanesborough there is a small harbor where we moored Jessica and set off on hired bicycles to explore the Royal Canal. From its summit near Mullingar the Royal Canal falls quickly and heads generally westward in the direction of Lough Ree until it comes within three miles of Derry Bay. Then, as if in search of less troubled waters for its terminus, it turns northwards and continues for another 13 miles until it eventually joins the Shannon near the village of Cloondara. Our original plan was to follow the tow-path to the west of the summit. But one look at the bicycles was enough to squash this in favour of a less ambitious ride.

Bicycles can be hired in most towns in Ireland. Raleigh has a Rent-a-Bike Dealer Network and, in theory, these machines should match up to a certain standard. But this restricts the point of hiring to larger towns. When we wanted a bicycle we were usually up against a less sophisticated system. For instance, the shop in Lanesborough offered bicycles at a fraction of the Raleigh rate. However, when we went to take them up on their offer we found the bikes were lying in bits on the floor of a shed at the back of the shop. Someone had started giving them an overall and re-paint but then lost interest. Interest was quickly regained with the prospect of business and we agreed to collect the machines at nine the next morning. Incidentally, that time, had been bartered down from "after ten" on their part to "by eight" on ours.

At nine we were sat on the doorstep waiting for them to open. By 9.15 we were tapping on the door, whistling, and pacing the pavement. At 9.30 I asked a neighbouring shop keeper what time competition from across the road usually started. I was told that they would surely be open in the next five minutes, a stock Irish answer if ever there was one. At ten we took to more purposeful banging on the door and hollering hellos up to the bedroom window. Just after 10.15 the door opened, but it was midday that we finally got onto the road and only then after doing most of the assembling ourselves.

Those bicycles were a torture to ride. One had a slow puncture, wobbly wheels, useless brakes, and saddles that must have dated from the days of penny-farthings. Diana had a. mock-up seat behind me and firm instructions to keep her legs stretched clear of the wheel and chain. But any bicycle is better than none at all and with the help of' a gale of wind behind us we rattled (quite literally) off the five miles to the locks at Killashee. The lock at Savage Bridge is the bottom one of two and the 44th on the canal. On the Royal there are 46 locks between Dublin and the Shannon, 10 of which are double ones. As there was no water in the canal I could walk about in the bottom of the lock chamber and inspect the gates and masonry at close quarters. All the levels to the west of the summit were drained when the canal was abandoned. However, abandoning a canal is not always as simple as it is in rural Ireland. Usually the channel has to be kept as a watercourse because factories along the banks have long standing agreements for the supply of water. Ironically, it becomes no more economic to close a canal than to keep it open. As with the locks I had seen beyond Dublin, all the masonry was in excellent condition. Only the gates indicated the years of neglect. They hung drunkenly and their balance beams had split and sagged to the ground. The bridge still carried the road over the canal and it was interesting to see that it had been built with the dressed stone to the side that faced the canal and irregular stonework on the side that faced the road. We were told by a man who farmed the surrounding land that he and his father before him had lived in the lock cottage, a family of' nine of them at one time, but they had never worked for the canal. As far as he could remember, the keeper from the next look looked after this one as well. Now the cottage is empty and fast becoming derelict.

In contrast, the cottage at the 43rd lock was one of the best kept that I have ever seen. It was freshly painted in white and blue and the old lady who lived there told us that she does it all herself. Her father had been the lock-keeper. "I reckon blue and white always went well together. I wouldn't have it any other way. They just call it 43rd Lock. The number is carved on the beams."

L.T.C. Rolt's account of his journey through the Royal Canal proved, as he says, to be its epitaph. We envied him that journey just as Rolt himself had envied Temple Thurston's good fortune in sailing through the now derelict Thames and Severn Canal. Our pencil-marked and memorized copy Rolt's book *Green and Silver* was a constant source of information and inspiration. We were therefore pleased to find that at the next lock his passage through the canal was remembered as if it was only yesterday. Our patron saint of canals travel suddenly became a thing of substance. While we sat on one of the balance beams eating our lunch, the lock-keeper lamented on the water highway that had previously passed within twelve feet of his front door.

The cottage garden that surrounded the 41st lock was a veritable miniature farmyard. Lock-keepers had always supplemented their income in this way, but now it was the hens and pigs, along with the donkey and the cow, that was the mainstay of their economy. From there on the locks are widely spaced out until the flight to the summit. We looked at the map, totted up the mileage, and decided that the bikes would never make it. We turned off at the next bridge and headed back to Lanesborough.

We did however see more of the Royal Canal when we reached Richmond Harbour the next day. Just below the Shannon lock at Termonbarry we turned Jessica into the channel that leads to the harbour and moored below what we had expected to be the first derelict lock. But the lock didn't look all that derelict and as we clambered up the bank we could see that a great deal of work was in progress. A new pair of top gates had been fitted and all was ready for new bottom gates. The canal above the lock was almost dry, but otherwise in a very different state to the overgrown ditches that we had cycled along the day before.

Since the early 1960's Norma and I had read everything about inland waterways that you can lay your hands on. We have lived afloat, been members of our local Branch of the Inland Waterways Association, campaigned and spent weekends helping to restore derelict canals, yet news from Ireland of this Government sponsored restoration scheme at Richmond Harbour had completely escaped our notice. It is telling tale of the remoteness of Ireland's inland waterways. Even now I am not sure how the project came about, and what was the driving force behind it. I believe the idea was first suggested at one of the Shannon Boat Rallies (an annual cruise in company that has become very popular) and was put forward by the Inland Waterways Association of Ireland. From then on the Board of Works carried the scheme through.

Beyond the lock the canal continues dead straight for a quarter of a mile before entering a deep cutting. The towpath follows the contours of the land high above. At least the cutting appeared deep at first glance, but its narrowness and low water in the canal may have exaggerated its depth. We followed the towpath until it petered out at a bridge and to get to the harbor from there we had to walk down the road to the village of Cloondara.

The explanation behind this baffling branch is that the Royal Canal emerges into quite a tangle of waterways. The canal we had walked along, and the lock that was being restored, was originally part of the main line of the Shannon Navigation. The first Shannon navigation scheme by-passed the rapids at Termonbarry by way of the canal and the River Camlin – a meandering reed fringed waterway that eventually rejoins the Shannon below Lough Forbes. The distance is less than two miles as the crow flies but more than twice by the waters of the Camlin. The present Shannon lock at Terrnonbarry dates from the major improvements made to the river during the 1840's. From then on the old cut served only to lead to the Royal Canal. The Admiralty Chart for Lough Ree includes the river up to Termonberry before the improvements were made. It has not been corrected since and hence historically all the more interesting. The chart shows that a canal bypassed a particularly narrow and rocky section of the Shannon below Termonberry, whereas with the improvements the canal and river were deepened and became one. It is still possible to navigate the River Camlin.

Richmond Harbour is a large expanse of water that can provide moorings for a considerable number of boats. Moreover, the moorings are fitting to their purpose and appear part of the natural scheme of things, which is something that a pontoon marina development can seldom achieve. Full credit is due to the Board of Works for the skill with which they have restored the harbour. Somewhere within that vast State machine there lurks good sense and ability, an attribute that is as valuable as it is rare. It is reassuring to lean over the bridge at Richmond Harbour and see that economics, function and aesthetics can still win the day. However, as I visited the harbour before work was finished I should perhaps reserve judgement in case of any last minute blunders. One innovation is the lamp standards, but they have been chosen with care. Rather than clumsy concrete or bogus wrought iron, they are slender tubular steel and scaled to their surroundings. When it comes to the business of something to tie up to, basically what moorings are all about, the Board of Works have sensibly avoided those that resemble clothes post ends and instead fitted a scaled down version of the mooring ring. The lock gates and balance beams are made of wood. A commendable decision but spoilt by inferior timber. In particular the foot-boards have warped to the extent that they unsafe. There is a dry dock in one corner of the harbor and that has also been restored. Finally, the buildings that line the quay side have been given a new lease of life; there are now houses, a shop, stores and warehouses.

When we got back to Jessica we found two converted Grand Canal barges moored next to us. We recognized them immediately for Weaver Boats and the Kennedy family has become a by-word on the Shannon. Their boats have been converted to carry lively people on a kind of adventure holiday that hundreds have become addicted to for life. To sign on as crew - one of twelve people of different ages, backgrounds and temperaments, to lend a hand with the cooking and the steering and working of the locks - may seem a strange recipe for an enjoyable holiday, but it is one that works unbelievably well. No one calls you out of bed in the morning or herds you around, the agenda is flexible and the pace is up to you. Furthermore, it's the best value for money holiday to be found anywhere. We came across the Weaver boats on other occasions during our travels on the Shannon. Each time the atmosphere aboard was so cordial, and the whiff from the galley so mouth-watering, that we always wished ourselves as one of the crew.

Soon after our journey through Ireland by river and canal I came across a Times article by Jill Tweedie titled, *Shannonigans*. Her take on cruising on the river is not that of an idyllic holiday but more of a refined form of torture, a Giles cartoon full of screaming kids and belting rain. I like boats and I like Ireland, and as Jill Tweedie pushes them both into the mud I suppose some loyal urge should have led to it being thrown overboard, instead of which I safely filed it away. Why? Because it's absolutely and hilariously true, every word of it! It serves to balance the tendency to remember only the best. But for the next day's happenings I did not need help from Jill Tweedie.

Looking back, misfortune, in the form of camp-fire cooking, started creeping in that very evening. The camp-fire came about through a whim of mine and a belief of Norma's that a pressure-cooker is the boom of small boat cooking, and that a greasy frying pan is the curse. Accordingly we carried no frying pan aboard Jessica. But as we had only a two burner primus stove and no oven, our menu could be rather on the dull side. It was my whim and fancy that we could brighten things up by going back, or at least part of the way back, to nature. An account of native cooking had caught my imagination, whereby food was simply wrapped in leaves and buried in the embers of a fire. Figuring that there might not be the right kind of leaves in Ireland we had stocked up with a roll of kitchen foil as a 20th century alternative. There is little room aboard a twenty foot boat and everything must pass a means test before being granted locker space. The foil had been squeezed in and to justify its existence we were committed to make use of it. At Lanesborough we had bought some sausages but by the next day they were threatening to go off. So that evening, below the lock that leads to the Royal

Canal, we began our cooking *plein air*. At first, Diana entered into the spirit of things but by the time she had scoured the towpath for suitable twigs, she become disenchanted. It took a lot of paraffin to get the twigs to burn and when they had caught hold, a lot of water to stop the flames setting fire to the grass and the hedges. We dare not wait until the fire got to the ember stage in case it went out, so while the flames were still going strong we wrapped the sausages in foil and tossed them in. A shift of wind funneled the smoke into Jessica but the resulting smell perked us up a little. Perhaps they might be edible after all. And they were, or at least one side of one end of one or two of them was.

The next morning we followed the barges towards Termonbarry Lock. By then the gale that we had managed to dodge on Lough Ree was blowing with all its might. Although the Shannon locks are large I was not sure that there would be room for both the barges and Jessica to pass through together. There is a large expanse of water below Termonbarry Lock and the wind was creating sizable waves at the entrance to the chamber. Rather than take a risk we moored Jessica to the landing stage below the lock and prepared to wait our turn. We watched the first of the bottom gates being closed, then, after a few moments indecision, the lock-keeper began to wave us in. We could not see into the lock from where we were moored but assumed that space had been made for us and we untied and set out. By the time we had got Jessica in line with the lock we had no distance left for further maneuvering as a gale of wind was hurrying us on. By then we could see that there was nowhere near enough room. I put the engine into hard astern, but there was no getting away from the inevitable. Jessica slewed around and drifted into the lock broadside. The mast, which in its lowered position sticks out over the stern, caught the lock gate with a sickening crash and Jessica's bow crunched into the rowing boats tied astern of the barges. Norma, who had been poised on the fore-deck, had somehow avoided being flung off. Jessica had been rammed sufficiently into the lock to enable the remaining gate to be closed behind her. At last the wind and sea were shut out. As the lock filled I surveyed the damage: broken mast crutch (but luckily not the mast), some bruised planking and the loss of our burgee - a burgee that had been flown on every mile of canal we had ever travelled. Once again we had fallen victim to the Shannon lock-keeper's practice of squeezing in all the boats they can at one time.

The only good thing that resulted from the lock episode was that with the mast now laid flat on deck we were able to sneak under the lift bridge at Termonbarry and so dodge having to pay for it to be lifted. At the jetty above the bridge we made a temporary repair to the mast crutch. The wind was howling angrier than ever with heavy black clouds for company. But we were in no mood to hang about at Termonbarry waiting for the weather to improve. We had something to eat and doggedly carried on.

For the next mile the east bank of the Shannon below Lough Forbes is littered with rocks. These are well marked and even in a high wind, which because of the river's twists and turns, comes at you from all directions, there is no danger providing that the engine doesn't fail. Fortunately, the engine never missed a beat, but the wind, with one terrific gust, lifted the inflatable dinghy clean out of the water until it flew like a kite at the end of its painter. It flopped back again upside down, no worse for its aerobatics except that the oars were left drifting downstream. To keep Jessica going straightforward along that stretch of river and in that wind had been difficult enough; to turn back in an attempt to pick up the oars was next to impossible. Even slowing down gave the wind the advantage, for without sufficient headway we would have been blown off course and into the shallows. Our oars were going on way while Jessica was forced to go the other, and for every second the gap between the two got wider.

That might have been the last that we could reasonably have expected to see of our oars had not the Shannon took such a crooked course towards Lough Forbes. Luckily they caught in the reeds at the next bend river, and at the same time, thanks to the Shannon's twists and turns, the wind was blowing Jessica off the rocks rather than onto them. Seizing our chance we nosed towards the shore. Here the water was more sheltered and we were able to hook the anchor between two big boulders. I stayed with the boat in case the anchor dragged while Norma, using a floorboard as a paddle, went off in the dinghy to retrieve the oars. To get to them she had to wade waist deep through the reeds and then I had to wade waist deep to unhook the anchor. As soon as we were on our way again the elements had their final fling with a downpour of torrential rain.

Soon we were anchored close to the reeds where the Camlin River leads off from the main line below Lough Forbes. The rain had settled in for the night and the wind was still with us. Even Jessica's cabin, normally cosy and cheerful, was damp and miserable with wet clothes everywhere. We could not get ashore as it was impossible to get the dinghy through the reeds. Not that it mattered, because on the map the nearest road was two miles away through water-logged fields and the nearest town twice as far again.

The next morning weak rays of sunshine tempted us on our way and we set off to cross Lough Forbes looking like a Chinese laundry with wet clothes strung out to dry. Lough Forbes is the first of a network of small lakes that the Shannon forms on its way down from Carrick. Nearly all of these lakes have a wide fringe of reeds around their shores. In some cases there are more reeds than open water. Because of this an ordinary map is not a reliable guide. But a virtue of the Shannon Guide is that it does show the reed line and therefore this publication comes into its own when navigating these waters. If you discount the water behind the reeds, Lough Forbes is little more than a wide stretch of the river.

Three miles above Lough Forbes is Roosky Lock. In the old days the Grand Canal boats used to enter this lock backwards when coming downstream. This was because there is often a fast flow on the river above the lock and the Bollinder engines, with which the boats were fitted, could not be easily made to go in reverse. In fact the Bollinder engine had no reverse gear as such. However, being a two-stroke, the engine could be enticed to run backwards, although in trying to achieve this there was a chance that the engine would stop altogether. By turning the barge well before the lock, and approaching stern first with the flow of the river, the engine could be put into forward to stop the boat and the rudder used to correct her course. On the River Ouse in England barges still use this technique to pass through the bridges at Selby.

To my mind Roosky is the dreariest town on the Shannon. It is situated a mile above the lock and consists of just one main street, some fly-blown shops and a meat factory. Nevertheless, it appears to be a popular stopping place for the hire-cruisers. To make the most of this bonanza the town has geared itself up with a "Crew's Bar" and Souvenir Shop. There is a lift bridge at Roosky but most boats can squeeze under with it in situ.

The beauty of the Shannon lies in its vastness. Because there are hundreds of square miles of waterway it is possible to turn a bend in the river and forget about Roosky. Therefore, to some extent, a Norfolk Broad scenario can be absorbed. But that is not to say that the river is completely immune from being ruined as many developers seem to think. At the time of our voyage pleasure boating on the Shannon was becoming business. In 1959 only 70 boats passed through the lock at Jamestown but by 1964 the figure was 1,672.

At this rate of development it is an illusion to think that there will always be a bit of unspoiled river left over. And it is no good waiting until the last square yard of open space has been gobbled up before deciding that something must be done. It is at this stage that some inspired planner should begin to think of the River Shannon, along with the Grand Canal and Barrow Navigation, in terms of a linier National Park. Unless that is done we may soon find that in sailing away from one Roosky we run straight into another.

The little harbour that serves the town of Dromod represents the Shannon waterside at its best. It is situated on the east shore of Lough Bofin and a navigation marker set on top of a cairn of stones marks the entrance. The harbour dates from the days when barges carried cargoes to the town. It was reconstructed by the Board of Works in 1969 and is a fine example of how the best of the old can be converted to serve present day requirements. In its original state the harbour was unsuitable for small boats because the fall from the quayside was too great. This has been overcome by stepping back the top half of the harbour walls so as to form a walkway. It is in the attention to detail that such schemes succeed or fail and in less capable hands the modification might have miscarried. Fortunately the Board of Works is expert at detailing. The bollards are in cast iron and a smaller version of the ship bollards to be found along many waterfronts. Around the edge of the walk-round is a hefty baulk of timber and the paving is made up of straight-forward stone slabs. Most important of all is the fact that where the harbour ends the country side immediately begins. There is no concrete waste land and no chicken wire fence.

Across from Dromod an arm of Lough Bofin stretches out to meet with Lough Boderg, and an arm of Lough Bnderg meets up with Lough Tap. The main line of the Shannon Navigation threads through this web of lakes, but it is possible, by sneaking out of the bottom corner of Lough Boderg and beneath Carranadoe Bridge, to reach Lough Grange and Lough Kilglass. We sailed in that direction the next day. For the first two miles beyond the bridge the channel is through a maze of reed beds and it is necessary to keep a careful lookout for the navigation markers. Occasionally the channel leads into an area of open water and when it does, the way out again is usually difficult to find. More than once we thought we had taken a wrong turning but then, at the last minute, a navigation marker would show up. Sometimes we were uncertain as to whether what we had sighted was in fact a marker, for frequently they are no more than the stump of a rotten post. Coming back was easier because then the bridge at Carranadoe kept coming into view and this gave us a sense of direction. But on the outward journey we had no landmark to help, just reeds and more reeds. The only other thing on the move that day was a heron and a kingfisher.

The original passage through these waters was to the quay at the head of Lough Grange and it was not until 1965, the beginning of the pleasure cruising era, that a short canal was cut to link with Lough Kilglass. Our intention had been to sail up to the Mountain River that flows into Lough Kilglass, for it is said to be an ideal mooring place, but by the time we had negotiated the maze of reeds low clouds and squalls of rain moved in and instead we went straight to the quay at Grange. The delight of these waters depends very much on the play of light, and rainy days are not the best on which to see them.

We tied up at Grange, for as far as we were aware, this was as far as it was possible to go. But we later learnt, from Hugh Malet's book *In the Wake of the Gods*, that by dinghy one can navigate up the Grange River and then on through a chain of small lakes to the village of Rodeen seven miles away. Had we have known this we would have spent the afternoon exploring that waterway, instead of which we walked to Strokestown, five miles away in the opposite direction.

By evening the skies had cleared and we started our return journey to the main line of the Shannon. Once or twice that we caught a glimpse of a red sail in the distance and when we came up to the quay at Carranadoe Bridge we found a yacht moored there. We learnt that it was part of the Kennedy hire fleet, a firm based at Jamestown a few miles further up river. Surprisingly the Kennedys were at that time the only firm on the Shannon that could offer sailing craft. Alas they have since sold off their fleet and motor cruisers are all that can be had. This is a sad state of affairs for the ideal way to cruise the Shannon is under sail. Yet the demand is for power craft, the faster and more rakish the better.

We had sunshine by the time we had left Lough Boberg behind the next day. Lough Tap is small and shallow and immediately beyond the Jamestown Canal leads off to the left. The canal, which is entered through Albert Lock, is one of the major engineering works on the Shannon. It bypasses a great loop in the river that is unnavigable because of rapids. It is however possible to continue up river to the quay below Drumsna, and to continue downstream from above the cutting to the bridge at Jamestown. For anyone with time to call at all the quaysides along the Shannon the round trip involves 400 miles.

Carrick on Shannon is only a few miles above Jamestown and we were surprised to find that we were the only boat there. This was contrary to what we had expected for the majority of the hire-fleets are based there. If there was one place on the Shannon that we expected to be crowded with boats, then that place had to be Carrick. The explanation soon became clear: we had arrived at Carrick midweek and all the hire-cruisers change hands at weekends. On Saturday the riverside at Carrick is like a Giles cartoon but from Sunday morning to Friday night everyone is elsewhere, hell-bent on putting in all the miles they can. From then on we began to plan our movements on the Shannon with this in mind. We found that we could have any harbor or anchorage virtually to ourselves, providing that we choose to go there at any time other than when the mass exodus was passing down from, or returning to, Carrick.

Two miles above Carrick the Boyle River flows into the Shannon. It is navigable to within 1½ miles of the town of Boyle and there is one lock at Knockvicar, just before Lough Key. Like the Shannon, much of the course of the Boyle is by way of interconnecting lakes. In terms of scenery, the Boyle is perhaps the more attractive of the two, for within its ten miles it has the variety that the Shannon lacks. Jessica sailed from Lough Drumharlow, which is all reeds with fields beyond, to Lough Key which is studded with islands and surrounded by mountains. It would take a hundred miles of the Shannon to achieve the same transformation. Admittedly when one tots up the height of the mountains from the map they do not amount to much. Coldly calculated the highest peak of the Curlew Mountains is only 828 feet, and the Bricklieve Mountains behind them can only just manage to scrape over a thousand. But mountains set their own scale, and it is not one that can be measured in so many thousands of feet. I believe that the person who christened them mountains cannot have been bothered with measurements at all. More likely, he viewed them from a boat on the waters of Lough Key. From that perspective they are mountains.

On the southern shore of lough is the Rockingham estate. The house, designed by John Nash, was destroyed by fire in 1957, but even as a ruin it looked an impressive sight as we approached from across the lake. Rockingham has its own harbor and it was there that we moored Jessica. It was there too that some of the romance of Rockingham began to fade. All about us bulldozers were at work making roads and a promenade. New buildings were being erected and on the lawn stood a batch of bogus tree-truck tables and seats. Behind them was a caravan park in the making.

The Lough Key Forest Park is a State sponsored scheme designed to keep Ireland's tourist attractions up to the Joneses of other lands. Forest parks, tourist lay-bys, picnic areas, caravan parks and marinas, are a recent and totally alien development in Ireland. The whole attraction of the country is that it abounds in grass verges and you can pull-in, picnic, or camp for the night, wherever you choose. One caravan pulled in off the road is perfectly fitting; a whole field full is a slum. And the term "Forest Park" does not befit Ireland. It is a misnomer and a misconception; they are a feature of Europe or the States. Visitors to Ireland should be prepared to come on the landscape's own terms and not expect to be herded in carpet slippers from one bit of prepared ground to the next.

At the time of our visit the Lough Key Forest Park should have been completed and open to the public, but because Ireland was in the grip of a cement strike, work was way behind schedule. We therefore had opportunity for a last unfettered look around. Near the harbour where we landed there was a second quayside. Both of them were connected to the house by long underground passages. This idea of keeping the mechanics of the estate out of sight was carried still further in the design of the house itself. All the kitchens and domestic quarters were contained in a great subterranean semi-circle behind the building. Rockingham also had its own canal system. We came upon an arm of this while on a walk around the lake shore. The channel was thick with water lilies and spanned by an ornamental bridge. The more extensive cuttings, which include a lock, were in part of the grounds that we could not get to. We tried rowing in from the lake, but reeds completely blocked the entrance. At Rockingham we once again had reason to envy L.T.C. Rolt, for at the time of his voyage the house still stood in all its glory and he was invited for tea.

From Rockingham it is only a short hop across the lake to where the river flows down from the town of Boyle. We left under a threatening sky and by the time we had moored to the jetty at the head of the navigation we were drenched. Before leaving England we had bought, in readiness for Ireland's climate, anoraks that were guaranteed 100% stormproof. They turned out to be nothing of the sort. After the first Irish downpour they began to positively soak up water rather than repel it. But trying to keep dry can be a more miserable business than actually getting wet and making the best of it. As we could not have got wetter had we decided to swim from Rockingham, we set out, there and then, and walked into Boyle.

On our way we passed a field full of caravans. Not the usual slick touring models but make believe Romany ones. They belonged to Gipsy Rover Caravans Ltd, and they offer a kind of holiday that is unique to Ireland. It is unique because only in Ireland is there still the quite country roads that make such slow-paced travel possible. You can hire a horse-drawn caravan and set out to explore counties Sligo, Mayo, Galway and Roscommon at the dizzy rate of twelve miles a day. Admittedly the caravans would make a true Romany winch and in any case Ireland is a land of Tinkers, not Romanies. On the other hand, there are few better ways of travelling through Ireland. One of the few better ways might be to hire a pony and trap from the same people and go off camping. Norma and I had this idea when, at a later date, we wanted to see the South of Ireland. But simpler still, instead of hiring a pony and trap we made a handcart, put our camping gear into it and set off. We leisurely walked in sandals or bare feet and with Diana along we could comfortably cover twenty to thirty miles a day. The need to cut down distances to accommodate children is a fallacy. Diana spent most of the journey running ahead picking wild strawberries. We kept to the minor roads, those shown as a narrow yellow or white line on the map, and in 200 miles rarely did anything more than a tractor pass us by.

At Boyle there are extensive remains of a 12th century Cistercian Abbey. In its time it was the most important in medieval Connaught and one of the finest in Europe. Unlike Cistercian foundations elsewhere, it is richly embellished. Many of the elaborate carvings have survived, in spite of considerable destruction by Anglo Normans and Cromwell's troops, some of whose initials can be seen carved on the timbers. Leading from the abbey are two underground passages; one to a neighbouring church, and the other to the shores of Lough Key. It is assumed that the passages were used for escape and as a store place for arms and provisions. All the little pamphlets that I collected from the counter of the local Tourist Office claimed that the Abbey was in an excellent state of preservation. But I cannot wholly agree. The three west bays in the south arcade of the nave have recently been blocked off for half their height by stone walls, left rough presumably in an attempt to blend in. Why? The only reason that I could see was to stop people getting in that way. If that is so it amounts to an act of vandalism to stop the vandals.

The town appeared suddenly around a bend in the road and we liked it, especially as a place to shop. All too often towns in Ireland consist of one wide main street - originally made wide to enable cattle to be driven through. But the river flows through the middle of Boyle and streets are sent scuttling off in all directions. In many Irish towns the local shops are being taken over by the grocery chains and modernized until one plate glass frontage looks very much like the next. But the shops in Boyle still have some character about them. Even the super-markets have been squeezed into existing buildings, rather than intruding with glass and concrete. In an early example of a department store we watched our change, in new pence, being whizzed from cashier to counter by means of a complex network of overhead wires. At the confectioner's biscuits could be bought pre-packed or alternatively, weighed out from tins set up beneath hinged glass lids on a mahogany display stand. Behind the counter in the chemist's shop stood row upon row of little drawers, and printed on them, in heavy serif capitals, the words Senna Leaves, Spices, and Comfrey, etc. On the wall above was a recent advertisement for Max Factor. The cycle shop had the very latest Japanese moped in the window, but an enamel sign above the door depicted an early upright machine and the caption: "The Raleigh All Steel Bicycle". Our purchases from one shop were wrapped in stiff brown paper and tied with string, while across the road they used self-seal polythene bags. Receipts ranged from elaborate letter-press bill-heads to chits from electric tills. Bygones and progress share the same shelf in the shops at Boyle and it makes shopping that little bit more exciting.

After the Boyle Navigation we turned northwards to tackle the last few miles of the Shannon. Soon after its junction with the Boyle the Shannon becomes a much narrower river and this, combined with the recent heavy rains we had been having, meant that Jessica had to push against a strong current. But from the junction to our objective, the town of Leitrim, was a distance of only four miles. We took trouble to sort out the most comfortable mooring that Leitrim could offer, for this was to be our base for the next fortnight whilst we went off to explore the abandoned Lough Allen Canal, and also the strangest of all Irish waterways, the long lost Ballinamore and Ballyconnell Canal.

For exploring these waterways we again needed to hire bicycles, but with the bone-shakers of Lanesborough still fresh in our minds I took the precaution of telephoning beforehand the nearest Raleigh Rent-a-Bike Agent to try to determine just what period of cycling history they were dealing in. M.T. Moran: Merchant, B.S.A. Motor Cycle Stockiest, Raleigh and Humber

Cycle Dealer, Hearse and Cars for Hire, etc. assured me that his machines were truly the best in all Ireland. Suitably impressed we set out to walk the five miles to his shop at Drumshanbo. We were not disappointed. Outside the shop two gleaming bicycles were propped up waiting for us, complete with pannier frames and a seat for Diana.

The Lough Allen Canal was constructed during the years 1818-22 and built to by-pass rapids on the river. The provision of this navigable link between the Shannon Navigation and Lough Allen was for the purpose of transporting coal, clay and iron from the western shores of Lough Allen near Artigna. However the canal did not succeed in developing the coal or iron works to any significant extent, nor did it generate any other worthwhile volume of traffic. The construction of a railway link from Dromod to Arigna towards the end of the last century provided a quicker and more convenient means of transport. The canal was abandoned in 1929 when the Ardnacrusha hydro-electric power station was put into operation. Lough Allen was needed as a storage reservoir for the scheme and consequently the level of the lake would be varied considerably.

The canal leads off from the Shannon at Battlebridge, about a mile above Leitrim. Battlebridge is the present northern limit of navigation on the Shannon and there is a quay below the lock. Above the lock the dry bed of the canal opens out into what was once a small basin. The towpath of the Lough Allen Canal is completely overgrown and to get to the second lock involved a long detour. The locks were built to take the Grand Canal size of craft and they were not enlarged during the subsequent improvements to the Shannon. Beyond the second lock we were able to take a small back road that followed the line of the canal for a mile or so. But there was not much to see. Indeed, had it not been for the familiar arch of a bridge and the fact that we were purposely searching for it, I doubt if we should have known that a canal had been there at all.

But one group of people who are well aware that the weed choked ditch was once a navigable waterway are the members of the Drumshanbo Branch of the Inland Waterways Association of Ireland. For many years they have been campaigning for the restoration of the Lough Allen Canal. They have the support of the Leitrim County Council and the Irish Tourist Board. In 1968 the Board of Works made a survey of the canal to access the feasibility of the project. Their report indicates that the navigation could be restored to Acres Lough, a small lake below Lough Allen, without undue difficulty at an estimated cost £30,000. The biggest job is likely to be clearing out the overgrown channel. If voluntary labour is forthcoming to help with this, as with canal restoration projects elsewhere, then it is likely that costs could be considerably reduced. For three quarters of a mile the canal has embankments constructed entirely of peat. Although peat is Ireland's most bountiful raw material it is not the best substance for building canal embankments. The report states that the embankments have subsided and show signs of fissures. As usual, the masonry of the lock chambers has stood up well and new gates are all that is required. It is therefore feasible that, in the not too distant future, Drumshanbo will be put back on the waterways map. But to restore the canal to Lough Allen is a different kettle of fish. A dam has been constructed across the upstream entrance to canal immediately beyond Drumshanbo Bridge. The dam, combined with deepening the river and dredging a channel into the deep waters of the lough, enables the Electricity Supply Board to draw down the level of the lake eleven feet lower than the old navigation level. The range between maximum flood level and low summer level is now five feet.

So that we might see something of Lough Allen, and also of the Arigna coal fields, we planned a cycle ride that would take us around the shores of the lake and up into the mountains that lie to the west of it. Lough Allen is the third largest of the Shannon lakes and its waters are the most expose. Away from the shore there are no islands to offer shelter and as we cycled the road that clings between Slieve Anierin and the fringe of the lake a westerly gale whipped up angry breakers onto the rocks below us. It was not so much the size of these seas that made one thankful to be on dry land, but their frequency. We went down to the edge of the lake and timed them; a wave crashed on that lee shore once every three seconds. The sky was dramatic. As each squall passed shafts of sunlight briefly highlighted patches of green three miles away on the far shore. Then all would turn black again and we'd grit our teeth in readiness for another soaking.

It took the morning to round the lake and it was early afternoon when began to climb the valley to Arigna. The road was narrow and every now and then we had to pull into the hedge to let a coal wagon pass. The railway to Arigna closed down in 1959. As one of the last surviving light railways in Ireland, the line had acquired an interesting collection of rolling stock from several extinct narrow gauge lines. Even in the 1950's up to 1,000 tons of coal a week was carried, most of it going the short distance to the power stations situated on the shores of Lough Allen. The Arigna coalfield outcrops on the flanks of the hills behind the town. The seams are so narrow and of such limited economic value that in the past their working was restricted to periods when imported coal was scarce. Wartime shortages did much to accelerate production and now the coal is used for power generation. At the time of our visit, the coalfields at Arigna stood second in production and employment capacity to the Castlecomer fields near Kilkenny.

Arigna is every bit a small mining town. The bank, the offices and the bars have an air of impermanence about them, makeshift affairs that are there just until the seams hold out. Corrugated iron is used a good deal in their construction, and that has always been the material of people who may have to one day move on. In the general store you can buy picks and shovels and pint size tin mugs. The coal is mined by driving horizontal passages into the hillside and hence there is no pit winding gear to be seen. Instead the entrance to each mine is marked by an aerial ropeway and a great escarpment of slag that has been removed from the workings. The ropeways carry the coal to loading shoots at the roadside.

Our map seemed to indicate a rough road that would take us along one side of the Arigna valley and back down the other. But it was only vaguely shown and in places appeared as if it might disappear altogether. As the journey involved a twelve mile wild and desolate circuit we inquired before leaving the town as to whether the road was passable. The answer was as non-committal as the cartographer's broken line on the map: sometimes it was and sometimes it wasn't. As the general verdict was that in summer it should be passable we decided to give it a try. We had to push our bikes for most of the first half. It was uphill and a gale of a wind was against us. The map showed a scattering of houses and even a school up on the mountainside, but they were all abandoned and derelict. The road doggedly carried on with no more than a few rough and boggy patches where it dipped from one side of the valley to the next. After a steep climb to the 1,000 foot contour it was then downhill with the wind behind us. For six miles we swooped down to Lough Allen and never once turned the pedals. At every coal shoot smiling black faces watched us go by.

The next day we began our exploration of the Ballinamore and Ballyconnel Canal. The canal was intended to provide the missing link between the Shannon and the waterways of Northern Ireland: a through route from Limerick to Belfast by way of Lough Erne and Lough Neagh, the Ulster Canal and the Lagan Navigation. The project was begun in 1846 and completed by 1859. But ten years later the canal was abandoned and during its brief working life no more than fifteen boats passed through. I doubt that any other waterway in Europe can claim such a sorry record.

The quay at Leitrim is situated a few hundred yards along the ill-fated canal. Beyond the quay the channel is thick with weed but we managed to row the dinghy up to the first lock.

There are sixteen locks on the waterway and eight of these climb the four miles between Leitrim and Lough Sour. The locks measure 82 feet by 16½ feet and there is a depth of 5½ft over the sills. We found that not only was the masonry of these looks in good condition but the metal work of the paddle gearing showed no appreciable sign of corrosion. The same applied to the gate collars. These were superbly made and had a flourish of decoration where the curve ends and the retaining arms begin. The squares for the windlass were as true as the day they were made and with virtually no traffic there had been no tow-ropes to scour groves in the bridge arches. Other than new gates, it appeared that little needed to be done to put the locks back into working order again. Beyond the first look the canal has been drained and, except for where the route is by way of lake or river navigation, this was the state of affairs throughout the 38 miles of the waterway,

It was easy for us to follow the canal to Lough Scur. A road runs close by and in some places it was possible to cycle along the towpath. Above Lough Sour the waterway becomes more elusive and it meant a considerable amount of pedaling to see precious little canal. There was no towpath, and the bridges we passed over had no provision for one. And then there are the lakes - six of them in all between the Shannon and Lough Erne - which involved long detours. I cycled the route to the east of

Ballinamore in one foul swoop, leaving Leitrim first thing in the morning and not getting back to the boat until after dark.

I was fortunate in having good weather and by the time I had reached St John's Lough, just west of Ballinamore, the sun was already hot on my back. Lough Scur is the summit level of the waterway and the canal begins its descent with one lock just before St John's Lough, and another one just after. To get to the second lock I cycled along what had once been the track of the Craven and Leitrim Light Railway. It was this railway that finally sealed the fate of the canal, for it served exactly the same localities. In 1887 the line from Belturbet via Ballinamore to Dromod (on the Shannon) was opened, and the following year the section from Ballinamore to Arigna was completed. The descent continues beyond Ballinamore with three locks that lead down to Garadice Lough. To construct this section the course of a river was completely diverted and the canal built along its bed. Garadice Lough, and the three smaller ones that follow, give a total of six miles of lake navigation. From then on the waterway continues to Ballyconnell by way of the Woodford River. Below Ballyconnell the navigation forms the border between North and South but because of the troubles I was unable to follow it further. I did however sneak across the border and into Northern Ireland to take a brief look at Lough Erne.

Lough Erne is a tangle of lakes and islands that stretch from Belturbet in the south to Belleek in the north. From end to end the navigation measures 52 miles and there is only one lock. But mere measurements convey nothing of the exciting cruising possibilities of the waterway, only a large scale map can tell you that. During the last century, most of the trade was by paddle steamers. They ran a regular passenger service and that continued until more recent times with excursion trips. One of the Erne steamers in fact passed through the Ballinamore and Ballyconnell Canal. The journey took three weeks and was only achieved by temporarily raising the levels so as to float the vessel over shallow sections. In 1780 an attempt was made to connect Lough Erne to the sea at Ballyshannon on the shore of Donegal Bay. One lock and a short section of canal were started but the project was soon abandoned. In recent years hire-cruisers have begun to operate on the lakes.

Anyone who has delved into the story of the Ballinamore and Ballyconnell Canal must surely come to the conclusion that to re-open the line would amount to the most exciting and far reaching of all canal restoration projects. It would do more than just put 38 miles of waterway back on the map, it would link two vast cruising grounds and in effect add hundreds of miles of waterway to each. Needless to say the Inland Waterway Association of Ireland is well aware of the possibilities and its Ballinamore Branch is specifically working towards that end. During our stay at Leitrim I met the Branch Chairman and Secretary. I found these two gentlemen, in company with the Assistant Secretary, in the Bar of the latter's Hardware Emporium. Seldom have I come face to face with such enthusiasm. Before I knew what was happening plans were being made to lift Jessica out and trail her from one navigable section to another. Alas, I had to persuade them that the boat, with all our gear aboard, would be too much for any trailer. Not in the least daunted they quickly came up with alternative schemes; either they would provide canoes the coming weekend or they would take us for a sail on Lough Garadice that very evening. But by the week-end we had to be on our way back down the Shannon, and for that evening we had already committed ourselves to other plans. I promised that another year we would come back and take them up on their offer. In the meantime my friends contented themselves with getting out from behind the bar large scale maps of the waterway and telling me of their progress to date.

The Branch was formed in 1967. Some of the members had

previously fought an unsuccessful but gallant campaign to save the Cavan and Leitrim Light Railway. Ironically, the passing of the railway was the first concrete step towards re-opening the canal. Two of the railway bridges had been built across the canal without navigable headroom, but as these were now obsolete the canal could once again have precedence. Initially the work of the Branch was directed towards stopping further decay. In doing this they were carrying out what had been the suggestion of a Commission set up to investigate the state of the canal eighty-five years earlier: "that steps be taken to prevent the banks of the canal and the masonry of the locks from falling into ruin, so that if in future it was required to reopen the navigation this could be done without too great an expenditure of money". Catching up on a backlog of eighty-five year's neglect was a mammoth task in itself. For two summers they set up work camps for twenty-five students who came from all over Europe to help. They concentrated on the line from Ballinamore to Lough Erne. As much of the distance is by way of lake and river navigation it offered the greatest mileage with the minimum of set-backs. To help publicise their campaign they temporarily raised the level of the Ballinamore stretch by putting stop planks in the lock below the town and held a boat rally there. Whilst working on the lock they found one of the pins that the bottom gates had hinged on. Like all the metal work along the canal it is in perfect condition. It now lives on a shelf above the bar and when the day comes for new gates to be fitted that pin will be put back in its rightful place. Only one or two of the lock chambers needed major work and nowhere had roads been lowered over the waterway, a frequent and costly difficulty met up with on many other canal restoration schemes. But there will undoubtedly be difficulties over water levels. To give the required depth for navigation, land around the lakes that has been reclaimed for almost a hundred years ago will have to be flooded.

At the time of our visit the Branch was raising funds for a detailed survey. In this way they will know the cost of restoration and they will not find themselves doing work which may afterwards have to be undone. The Tourist Boards both North and South of the border had expressed considerable interest in the waterway and hope was running high that soon the project could be got off the ground. There was only one cloud on the horizon, but soon after our visit that cloud grew until it over shadowed all else.

It is impossible now to think of the Eallinamore and Ballyconnell Canal without linking it to the turn of events in the North of Ireland. The line lies precariously between North and South and the troubles of the early 1970's halted plans for reviving the waterway route between the two lands. But I believe it is only a set-back and that in the end the venture will go forward with a renewed vigour and purpose. Over the last two decades voluntary canal restoration projects have captured the imagination of the public. In an age of strikes on the one hand and apathy on the other, thousands of people from all walks of life have freely given their spare time to clear mud choked ditches. In doing so, many of the volunteer navies have found a new purpose to life. If the people of the North and the South of Ireland could together become passionately involved in such a project, then the restoration of the Ballinamore and Ballyconnell Canal is likely to be the greatest social adventure of our time.

In the meantime not all stands still. A recent book *The Ballinamore and Ballyconnell Canal* by P.J. Flanagan gives a complete history. And by the same author there is a book about the Cavan and Leitrim Railway.

The day we left Leitrim Norma was given a sack of vegetables from the lady at the pub and an old man from the village brought a banana for Diana. He told us that if ever we returned we would be welcome in any house there. Such is the friendliness of the Irish. Since our voyage we spent two years living and working in Ireland. Our stay was through the darkest days of the troubles when the newspapers reported nothing but violence and hatred from these shores. Yet during all of our time there we received nothing but friendship. In return we developed a great and overwhelming love for the people of that land.

THE LOWER SHANNON

It took five days to leisurely sail back down the Shannon. On the fifth day the Slieve Bloom Mountains began to pile up on the skyline and by evening the bold outline of the canal hotel at Shannon Harbour was in sight. Soon we were covering new ground. Banagher was only a few miles away but we did not approach any nearer that night. Through the gathering dusk we could hear the clatter of the town's temporary Bailey bridge and decided that a back-water of the river would make a more peaceful mooring.

We sailed down to the town the next day. The moorings, has we had imagined, were near the bridge. But despite the racket we were attracted towards it for beneath the temporary Bailey structure the old Shannon swing bridge remained intact. Even though it had seen better days, there could be no doubt that here was a superb piece of engineering. The design is based upon an interlocking arch, the spans of which swing to a position parallel to the navigation to allow the boats to pass. The bridge and the elegant castings for the winding mechanisms is a fine testimony to the skill of the 19th century ironworker. The magnificent bollards nearby are likely to be the work of the same hand. Upon them are the words, Shannon Commission and the date, 1844. Cast in bold letters upon the bridge itself are the words *Thomas Rhodes, Engineer*. Thomas Rhodes first gained prominence as an assistant to Thomas Telford on the Caledonian Canal and later worked in collaboration with him on the Menai Bridge and St. Katherine's Docks. It was while working as resident engineer at St. Katherine's Docks that Rhodes designed and built the prototype upon which the Shannon bridges were based. The bridge keeper's hut was also still standing and left just as it was when the bridge had been swung for the last time. Under the window was a built-in desk and beneath it a high stool. On a shelf stood two ledgers, a red lantern, oil can, bottle of ink, a pin stuck with papers, and a calendar for 1966.

Ten years before that date the swing bridges of the Shannon had represented an impending doom to the navigation. They needed replacing and an effort was made to substitute them with fixed spans that would have been far cheaper to construct. However, this would have made the navigation of the Shannon impassable to anything larger than a rowing boat. It was then that the Inland Waterways Association of Ireland was formed and their first task was to persuade the authorities to retain headroom. New vertical lift bridges, such as the one at Termonbarry above Lough Ree, are a result of their success. The old bridge at Banagher remains because even in its closed position there is adequate headroom beneath it. It would however be fitting if this last example of the Shannon swing bridges could be preserved. There could be no finer monument to the skill of those who built the navigation and moreover, to the foresight of those who fought for its future.

I discovered another piece of early ironwork on the quayside at Banagher, but this time remarkable for its origins rather than its design. It was a hand crane, and the maker's plaque bore the words: *Thomas Smith & Son, Steam and Electrical Crank Works, Rodley, Nr. Leeds*. The village of Rodley lies on the banks of the Leeds and Liverpool Canal, and it is likely that this piece of machinery took the very same route to Banagher as ourselves. It would have been loaded onto a barge and taken by canal to Liverpool. From there it would have been sent by sailing ship to Dublin, and then consigned via the Grand Canal to the Shannon. A hundred years separated our respective journeys.

Below Banagher the Shannon is riddled with islands and backwaters and it is necessary to keep a careful lookout for the navigation markers that lead to Victoria Lock. We passed through the lock in company with a number of hire-cruisers. The crew of one of the boats neglected to keep a watch on their ropes as the level dropped and before they realised what was happening their craft was strung at an alarming angle. The water had already fallen to the extent that no one could get off the other boats to help, and no amount of shouting could attract the look-keeper. He was looking in the other direction and still winding up the paddles. It was some quick action with a bread-knife that saved the day. The ropes were cut and the boat splashed upright again. A golden rule is never to make ropes fast when falling in a lock. The free end should be around a bollard so that it can be payed out as the level falls. But ropes are not all that necessary when descending. There is no force of water and a boat will usually lie quietly alongside. At the same time it is the responsibility of whoever raises the paddles to keep a careful eye on things so that if anything going wrong they can be immediately lowered. In my experience the Shannon lock-keepers are at times negligent in this respect.

Portumna, a small market town situated at the head of Lough Derg, lies eight miles downstream from the lock. Leading off from the river at that point is a short branch canal, at the end of which is an excellent little harbor within easy walking distance of the town. I say excellent in a purely utilitarian sense, for the quaysides are spoilt by phony chain link fencing, fussy flower pots, and the wrecks of a couple of cars. While there we put the mast up in readiness for Lough Derg. But no sooner had we done that than a gale blew up and kept us weather-bound for three days.

During our enforced stay at Portumna we met up with another yacht from England. She sailed into the harbour with her gleaming white hull festooned with motor tyres. We guessed that she had come through the Grand Canal and afterwards learnt that the father and son crew had made the journey from Dublin in three days flat! Furthermore, they had set out from England with the intention of sailing the Grand Canal and the Shannon, and back again to England in a fortnight. The Irish say that it takes a week to slow down an Englishman to their pace of life, and a fortnight to slow down an American. I believe that these particular Englishmen were beginning to learn. They became quite content to sit back and wait for the weather, and when we saw them again a week later they were still on Lough Derg.

By the end of the second day, which was a Saturday, quite a flotilla of craft had built up. It consisted of two sea going yachts, one of the large hotel boats, a Grand Canal barge, and a converted 40 foot motor fishing vessel. In each case the skippers thought it prudent to wait for better conditions before venturing out onto the waters of Lough Derg. Yet on that same afternoon four hire cruisers set out from their base at Killaloe in the south and crossed the lake to Portumna. Not one of those aboard the boats had any sailing experience worth mentioning. They had set out in a belief that there is safety in numbers and had crossed the lake more by luck than management. This was made clear as they approached Portumna Bridge that evening. The bridge is the lowest on the river and needs to be swung for almost every craft. With a gale of a wind behind them these boats approached at full speed, presumably under the impression that the bridge was worked by a magic eye and would swing open for them at the last moment. But the Portumna Bridge has no such sophistications. It is swung by hand and to swing it takes a long time. Each boat brought up with a crash against the girders of the bridge and one crew member ducked only just in time to escape being decapitated.

I went to help the bridge keeper and his wife. The bridge at Portumna is an odd one out and the navigation section consists of one huge swinging span. As I have said, it is wound round by hand, and if anything on the Shannon needs electrifying then this is it. To swing the bridge at the best of time is hard work, but to do the job against a gale of wind took the all the strength that the three of us could muster. In closing the bridge I foolishly let go of my handle. Immediately the bridge keeper made a grab for it. He told me that in a gale you would never be able to stop her! As for the hire-cruisers that we had just passed through, the bridge keeper said that they just don't see the danger in it, and you can't tell them.

Lough Derg is the largest and loveliest of the Shannon Lakes and the most treacherous. During our time on the lake the weather was never settled and we sailed across it in fits and starts, dodging from one sheltered anchorage to the next. When it comes to the hazards of sailing the Shannon, Joshua Slocum, the first man to sail alone around the world, expressed it best when he wrote: 'the sea does not suffer fools for long"!

We made an attempt to get away the next day, but by the time we had reached the first of the lake buoys the wind and sea were dead against us and we made little headway. We ran back to shelter under foresail alone and anchored for the night in a reedy channel that separates a small island from the mainland. The following morning we managed to get as far as Rosemore Bay. This is on the west shore, about seven miles down the lake from Portumna. There was once a quay at Rosemore, but it is now in ruins. The recommended anchorage lies just off the quay, although to get more shelter we moved further in nearer the reeds. This was a mistake, for there are submerged rocks and all we did was exchange one hazard for another. If we had looked more carefully at the reeds that had tempted us in we would have been forewarned. There are two types of reeds on the Shannon and they indicate the suitability of an anchorage. There is the tall rush, light green in colour and with numerous blades growing from its main stem. This reed has a feathery top, rather like a miniature specimen of pampas-grass. Its presence represents an area of rocks and shallow water. On the other hand, the type of reed that is darker in colour, not quite so tall, and has hollow stems surmounted by brown turfs, indicates a soft bottom and comparatively deep water.

I rowed ashore at Rossmore Bay and went off in search of a shop. I did not find one, but what I did find was that the countryside was by no means as flat and monotonous as a glance at the map would suggest. A road lined with trim hedges led me through rich rolling farmland and passed whitewashed cottages. It was like an Irish travel poster, except for the sky. In the distance, mountains and dark clouds merged together and it was difficult to tell one from the other.

That evening we made the most of a calm spell and pushed on another six miles to Williamstown. Enroute we passed

Illaunmore, the largest island on Lough Derg. A marker buoy thereabouts goes by the name of Benjamin. It is a big black can shaped buoy and set on top of it is a white concrete bust - presumably Benjamin himself! The harbour at Williamtown is privately owned and visiting craft must tie to a dolphin off shore. In view of the unsettled weather it may appear folly that we choose such a seemingly exposed mooring. But the weather was at least settled in the fact that it was all coming from the west, and Williamstown, being on the western shore, was sheltered from that direction. However, we were none too pleased at having to hang on to a slippery staging when a peaceful haven was but a few yards away. There was a solitary motor boat in the harbour and I rowed over to ask if we might moor there for the night. The answer was an unequivocal 'NO'. Obviously the occupants of the desirable residences that look down on the lake prefer to keep water gypsies at a safe distance.

We set the alarm clock to wake us at first light the next morning. Very often the wind comes up with the sun and we hoped that by making an early start we could sneak around to Mountshannon. This we managed to do, but only just, for soon the wind was blowing as hard as ever. Fortunately, there can be no better place to be weather bound. The harbour is sheltered and the village is one of the most attractive on the Shannon. The main street is shaded by leafy trees and at the end stands a Youth Hostel. As Norma and I had once worked for the Youth Hostel Association in England we were interested to see the Irish equivalent. On a subsequent journey through Ireland we stayed at a number of hostels and found them to be, like Youth Hostels everywhere, good, bad, and indifferent. Too often the Youth Hostel movement confuses simple accommodation with squalid accommodation, and increasingly the spirit of Youth Hosteling - to cater for persons of limited means travelling under their own steam - gets caught up in the need to secure lucrative block party bookings. However, one becomes expert at weighing up a hostel from outside: the state of its grounds, dustbins, curtains at the window, petty notices on the door, paintwork, etc. From what we could see the hostel at Mountshannon is to be recommended.

At the other end of the main street is a blacksmith's shop and through the open door we watched a horse being shod. Because Ireland is essentially an agricultural nation, and a little behind times, it is possible to witness rural crafts that have either died away altogether or become affected museum pieces in other lands. This was the first time in our lives that we were seeing in the flesh this basic facet of the blacksmith's craft. The atmosphere was that of an ancient ritual. The smell of burning hoof, the glow of red-hot metal, the incomprehensible words that passed between worker and local onlookers and the wows and oies to the horse. The floor of the shop was just dust and straw and there was no glass in the window opening. An anvil, a forge, a rough bench with an old leg vice, nails in the wall with horse shoes hanging from them and everywhere pieces of rusty metal. It was a scene that cannot have changed in a hundred years. Except that is, for one thing. In a corner stood the bright red box and control knobs of an electric arc welder.

One other daily activity at Mountshannon was swimming instruction. A pool has been constructed near the harbour and each day two instructors went down there with parties of school children. Although we had happened to hit upon a special life-saving week, and in consequence the pool was busier than usual, I was nevertheless assured that it was far from deserted at other times. How much better it is for a town to accept their waterfront in this way rather than turning their backs on it. So often the cry is for a stretch of canal to be filled in to make it safe, whereas what are really needed are positive initiatives for safely living with water.

From Mountshannon we sailed to Scarriff, a town at the end of an arm that stretches west from the main course of Lough Derg. The town is set back from the lakeside and is finally reached by navigating 1½ miles of canalised river. For most of the way the river wanders about as if lost and the navigator has to steer a tortuous course to reach the town. At the last bend of all we had a moment of panic for we noticed, almost too late, that electricity cables crossed the channel. From our position in the cockpit it seemed as if the mast must surely catch them. In an effort to stop in time we threw the engine into astern and ran Jessica into the reeds. The people standing on the quay could not understand what all the fuss was about. From their vantage point, as we later saw for ourselves, it was obvious that we would clear the cables by 20 feet or more.

The town of Scariff is dominated by a chipboard factory. Chipboard, together with hardboard and plywood, has revolutionized the joinery business. The chances are that your sideboard, if manufactured within the last fifteen years, has chipboard beneath its teak veneer. It is an economical and stable alternative to natural timber. It is made by reducing every cubic inch of a tree to chippings and then bonding them together again in sheet form. Because its ingredient is 99% soft wood a great deal of it is made in Ireland and used in Ireland, and a considerable amount is exported. I asked if I might look around the factory but as no one had ever made that request before it put the receptionist in a spin and I eventually dropped the idea. The Irish Tourist Board lists firms that may be visited: there are potters, lace-makers, weavers and brewers, but not chipboard manufacturers.

It was while we were at Scarriff that the weather gods decided to throw in a few settled days of summer. We made the most of this by escaping from the lee of the land and sailing over to the eastern shore of the lake. Our objective was Garrykennedy, a harbour where Sandlark, the last of the Shannon turf boats, was reputed to lie.

The remains of a castle stand prominently on the breakwater at Garrykennedy and the harbour was built from stone taken from the ruin. Like all Shannon harbours it is tiny when compared with those around our coasts, but perfectly in scale with these inland seas. It is a popular mooring and during our four days there many boats stopped by. Most were hire-cruisers and crewed by foreigners, in particular, Germans, French, and Swiss. In the small bay alongside the harbor lay the black hulk that was the reason for our visit.

The Sandlark was sunk in a few feet of water and my days were spent rowing out to her to take photographs and measurements. She was the last of a particular type of vessel and to the best of my knowledge no detailed record of them exists. It seemed that I had arrived only in the nick of time for plans were afoot to break up the vessel. Her wreck was considered to be a nuisance and an eyesore. However, I had not been there long before the cunning villagers offered to sell her to me, thinking as how she would make a lovely house boat. When I declined yet continued to show interest in her remains they then thought there might be something in that and before I left plans were being made to preserve her as a tourist attraction. But the Sandlark has not the making of a second Cutty Sark. She is the descendant of a type of craft evolved to trade upon the wide waters of the Shannon; bluff bowed sailing barges that carried cargoes of turf. The boats were sloop rigged with an average length of 50 feet. Their carrying capacity worked out at about a ton per foot.

The Sandlark is of uncertain age and has undergone a number of alterations during her lifetime. Not least of these was when she was cut in two and lengthened by ten feet. There is an old lady living in the village who remembers this being done. Two tradesmen did the job and she used to take cups of tea down to them. At first I found it hard to believe how anyone could contemplate the task of lengthening a vessel of that size. Yet there was indisputable evidence, both eye-witness and structural, that this had been done. Later I learnt from Basil Greenhill's book, *The Merchant Schooners* that even larger and more complicated hull forms had been altered during the hey-days of wooden ship building. Another major alteration was the installation of a Bolinder semi-diesel engine. It was started by compressed air and was one of the first in Ireland to be fitted with this innovation. The installation of the engine can be dated to the years 1925-30 when the Ardnaorusha Power Station was being built. Local boats were contracted to carry materials for its construction and a lot of money was earned. Carrying for the Germans, the people of Garrykennedy called it, an expression that had me puzzled until I remembered that it was a German firm that had acted as consultants for the scheme.

The principal dimensions of the Sandlark are: length stem to stern post 60ft 7in, extreme beam 13ft 9in and depth of hold 6ft. She has a transom stern and her bows are similar to those of a Thames Sailing Barge. This, together with no noticeable sheer and only a slight deck camber, gives the boat a rather ungainly appearance. There is a cabin in the bows and the engine is under a large hatch at the stern. No division remains between the main hold and the area under the aft hatch and stern deck, but it appears that the engine took up a prodigious amount of cargo space. The main hatch measures 30ft 6in x 8ft 6in. The planking is of two inch oak, iron fastened onto frames spaced at 18inch centres. All trace of the mast and rigging have disappeared.

It was a fire that brought an end to the Sandlark in the early 1950's. A relief crew had brought her into Garrykennedy with a cargo of empty porter barrels and the fire started just after they had left the boat for the night. The villagers were quickly on the scene and they sank the boat to stop the flames spreading. Very little damage had been done but trade was not what it had once been and the boat was never repaired.

Hauled out on the side of the bay are the remains of three other turf-boats, one of which was of composite construction, i.e., wood planks onto steel frames. In fact, Garrykennedy had been the home port of eight turf boats at the turn of the century and the old people in the village could remember those days. William Donlon, brother of Michael Donlon who was mate aboard the Sandlark, remembers that there was always a smell of tar about the place and whenever you lifted your head a boat could be seen sailing by: "They had bows like a duck, and a duck doesn't make any commotion in the water now does it?" The boats were hauled out for repairs with a winch set up on the shore of the lake below the village. They made and mended their own sails and applied hot tar to preserve them. To each boat there would be a crew of three and they might be away for up to six weeks at a time. Nan Lynch is sister to James McGrath who had owned the Sandlark. She took me to see a shed in her garden that was made from the frames and planking of boats. There were bits of boats everywhere. She showed me an old block taken from the rigging of the Sandlark and a photograph of the Swan under full sail. Ruth Delany mentions in her book, *The Canals of the South of Ireland* that when the vessels were under sail the angle of heel was measured by the number of sods of turf that were under water. They were good old days, agreed Nan and Willy, "the days of - now let me think - the Swan, the Lily, the Foam, the Lady of the Lake, and the Sandlark".

Each evening after my work aboard the Sandlark Norma and I headed for Jim Ryan's Bar. Normally a brewery could not depend upon our custom to keep in business, for long ago we had become disillusioned with the chromium plated, bogus olde-worlde, juke-box and television pubs of England. Many of the Bars in Ireland can be just as dismal, for all the blarney that says otherwise, but Jim Ryan's is an exception. Diana came with us too, for there is no law in Ireland to say that children cannot enter pubs. Perhaps it is the inclusion of family that makes the difference and also the fact that many of the pubs in Ireland are also the general store. Packets of Persil jostle with bottles of Guinness on the shelves behind the bar and Mrs. Ryan beamed over her customers - old men, young men, mothers, daughters and a brood of little ones - like a benevolent grandmother. Some sat on the hard wooden benches against the walls and others on the upturned porter barrels around the bar. Many more were left standing. The bar wasn't clinically clean, the ceiling was smoked to a deep yellowish brown and the floor was like that of a farmyard, but it was alive. And it was especially alive on Saturday nights when there was dancing and singing to the accompaniment of the fiddle, accordion and spoons. All too soon, Jim Ryan would start banging his stick. Time was being called.

It was during an evening at Jim Ryan's Bar that I was cajoled into buying a raffle ticket in aid of the local development committee. But having already seen some of the committee's work I was not at all sure that I wanted Garrykennedy to be developed. The harbor was well on its way to being spoilt. A red and black concrete crash barrier has been erected and a lot of earth moving was in progress. Nan Lynch does not like the barrier at all. "I dare not say much for they tell me it will be safer for the children, but generations of children have been raised here without the help of that barrier. And it was lovely before they did the tipping, all trees and big rocks where you could sit. But they say it will bring tourists and I'm called a square for not wanting such things".

After leaving Garrykennedy we rounded Parker's Point, one of the deepest and most exposed parts of the lake, and headed for Killaloe. The town is situated at the most southerly point of Lough Derg and the approach lies between the Slieve Bernagh and the Arra Mountains. Before the Ardnacrusha Power Station was built the navigation at Killaloe was by way of a lock and side canal, but the subsequent flooding of the lower reaches had made this obsolete. However, the canal still remains and serves as an excellent linier harbour for the town. There is a fixed bridge soon after the entrance to the canal and Jessica's mast meant that the most coveted moorings by the lock were bared to us. But all that separates the canal from the river is a narrow wall and thanks to Jessica's shallow draught we were able to moor to the outside of this and thus secure for ourselves the best position of all.

The entrance to the Killaloe Canal is known as the Pierhead, a name that originates from the days of steam boat services on the Shannon. I was reminded of those days when casually glancing at a display of picture postcards outside the souvenir shop in Killaloe. In amongst the usual lurid sunsets and pictures of donkeys and Irish dancers, was a much more subdued study that showed a white hulled steamer passing beneath Banagher Bridge. A top hatted gentleman stood in solitary state on the aft deck. Only the last two letters of the ships name were illegible but from the list of steamers that plied upon the Shannon I was able to identify her as being the Countess of Cadogan. The card was a veritable collector's piece and must have been part of some old stock that had recently come to light. From the dress of those depicted, the colouring technique, and the fact that careful scrutiny revealed that the steamer was moored stationary for the shot, dated to the photograph to the late 19th century. This was confirmed by researching the fortunes of the Shannon Development Company, a venture set up to provide a passenger and light goods service on the river. The company was formed in 1891 and when fully expanded possessed six fine vessels, three of which were capable of carrying 200 passengers at a speed of 15mph. The Countess of Cadogan was one of the three and together they operated a daily service between Killaloe and Athlone. But by 1903 regular services were suspended and the vessels operated in the summer months only. In 1906 the Fairy Queen, one of the smaller steamers that had worked north of Athlone, went to operate on Lough Corrib in County Galway. She was replaced in 1913 by the Countess of Cadogan. The Shannon steam boat services were suspended at the outbreak of War in 1914 and never resumed.

In Killaloe Cathedral is a memorial to John Granthan. The plaque states that it was he who "first surveyed the River Shannon with a view to improving it and of him having been the first to introduced Steam Navigation on its waters in the year 1825". The vessel was the Marquis Wellesley which was built at Tipton in Staffordshire. After being reassembled at Liverpool, she crossed the Irish Sea en-route to Lough Derg. Another steamer that had to make her initial journey from the builders in sections was the Lady Lansdowne. She was built at Birkenhead in 1833 and re-assembled at Killaloe for she was too big to pass through the canal from Limerick. With a length of 133 feet she was the largest river steamer ever to be seen in Ireland. Her remains were discovered at Killaloe in 1957. She lies close to the east bank under three feet of water. I located the wreck from the dinghy but silting had hidden most of her hull.

While rowing back from prodding at the remains of the Lady Lansdowne I paused to admire a large motor yacht moored a short distance downstream from the wreck. She was of an age that knew nothing of glass-fiber and a fine example of the shipwrights' craft. I learnt that she was a floating home for the family that owned her and had only just undergone an extensive refit. Little did I imagine that within less than an hour she would be a total loss.

We had just sat down for dinner when we heard a dull thud. My first reaction was to look towards the bridge; it was narrow and vehicles frequently came close to colliding. But as there was no commotion in that direction I began to scan the far river bank. At first I could see nothing amiss, but then noticed a puff of smoke above the motor yacht. On looking through the binoculars I was shocked to see that her coach-roof had been blown off. Within seconds the whole boat was engulfed in a sheet of flame. Along with what seemed like half the population of Killaloe I ran across the bridge to the far shore. I feared that those aboard her would have been blown unconscious by the blast and trapped inside. Fortunately that was not so. In the few seconds between the explosion and the fire that followed they had managed to escape. However, the chance of saving the boat was hopeless. Within minutes she was an inferno and then the petrol tanks caught, erupting with a great roar like the flame from a giant blow-lamp. An attempt was made to scuttle the boat but the heat was too intense for anyone to get close enough for more than a quick and in-effective jab with an axe. I then realised that the mooring ropes were burning through and she would soon begin drifting towards Jessica. While the others tried to secure her with chains. I ran around to be ready for some rapid berth shifting. Fortunately the boat did not drift and soon a fire engine could be seen crossing the bridge. But only slowly, for there was a donkey and cart ahead of it!

It was later established that the cause of the fire was a butane gas explosion, sparked off by a flash between electrical contacts on the engine starter system. The danger of using bottle gas aboard boats is not generally understood. The gas is heavier than air and any leakage can lie undetected in the bilge. Out of all the boats that I have come in contact with over the years not one has been lost at sea, but three have been totally destroyed by butane gas explosions.

In terms of cruising the Shannon, Killaloe is as far south as boats go. But the navigation extends to the estuary at Limerick. The Ardnaorusha Power Station, along with one of the deepest locks in Europe, is along that section of the river. Such were the tales of hazards on the lower reaches that we decided to leave Jessica at Killaloe while we went by bus to visit Limerick and the power station. In retrospect I do not believe that the journey is as hazardous as is it made out to be. The danger is of fast currents in the head and tail race canals. However, for most of the summer months the turbines only run at slow speed and the flow is not excessive. Nevertheless, I would not recommend the passage, tempting as it may be, unless a boat wishes to gain access to the estuary. At Limerick the river is tidal and mooring would be difficult.

After months of travelling at a top speed of 5 mph the journey to Limerick by bus put us in a state of nervous tension. Although I am certain that the driver drove safely the runs downhill seemed positively suicidal and we were glad to find our sea-legs again on the canal bank at Ardnacrusha.

The channel was straight and wide and had sloping sides like a ship canal. It was spanned by the power station and we walked towards it along recently mown banks. There was very little in the way of pylons or cables to give the game away. The scene was a rural and we came to the conclusion that there are worse ways of generating power. We first went to a group of cottages - yes cottages, not red brick factory houses - in search of the lock-keeper, but no one was at home. Eventually he found us rather than we found him and certainly we were welcome to have a look around.

Ardnacrusha Lock is within the power station complex and situated at the end of the turbine house. It is kept under lock and key and we followed the lock-keeper through clanging gates and along echoing corridors, just as prisoners follow the jailer in the dungeons of radio sound effects. The lock consists of two chambers and together they fall 110 feet. We looked into the depths of the top chamber first. It was empty and the perspective of the access ladder ran out into almost nothing. The lock gates are of the guillotine type and boats pass from one chamber to the next through a hole in the dividing wall. All was silent except for a distant hum and the eerie amplified sound of a drip. A lift dropped us down to the level of the bottom chamber. Above the lower gate is the control room and from there we watched the intermediate gate being lifted to reveal the dark opening that leads to the top chamber. From the detachment of the control room I found it difficult to appreciate the vast scale of Ardnacrusha Lock. Then it dawned on me: an insignificant dot that I had been looking down upon was the look-keeper's assistant sweeping up.

At Limerick we saw something of the original line of the Shannon Navigation. The first lock leaves the river not far from the centre of the city and we were surprised to find that it is still kept in working order. Work on the navigation between Limerick and Killaloe was begun in 1755 under the direction of Thomas Omer, but it was still incomplete fifty years later and only doubtfully passable by 1829. The first canal cut rejoined the river after about a mile then a second cut extended for five miles. In total there were eleven locks, three of them being double. As with the Lough Allen Canal, these locks were not enlarged during the river improvements of the 1950's. In the Robertstown Canal Museum I saw a map of the Shannon prepared by the Irish Inland Steam Navigation Company in 1830. On the Limerick sheet the line of the canal and the position of looks are clearly shown and mention is made that a packet boat plies daily to and from Limerick and Killaloe. We noticed that the first lock was unusual in having an inset convex radius carved along the edge of its coping stones. Little did we realise that this ornate flourish was to provide an important clue in piecing together the history of another waterway later in our voyage.

Travelers of the 1970's have no steam packet upon which they can return from Limerick to Killaloe. Instead we had to wait for the bus. It is an infrequent service and we had two hours to spare before we could make the return journey. To while away the time we walked along the quays and visited the museum. Just below the lock the navigation follows the course of the Abbey River and passes beneath two low bridges. This must be the most difficult stretch of all to navigate. Unless the tide is timed just right there will either be not enough water to float the boat, or too much so as to obstruct headroom. The quayside continues until the docks and beyond there the river broadens out into a wide estuary. Limerick Museum Art Gallery and Library are all combined, and practically share the same room. Although the collection was not by any means extensive, its short comings were more than made up for by an enthusiastic member of staff. The lady personally guided us from one exhibit to the next and enlightened the way with snippets of information. Her commentary was not one that had been learnt long ago and recited parrot fashion ever since. It was alive with a wealth of observation that all the time was stumbling on new discoveries. Our tour came to a fitting climax before a picture of the Limerick waterfront painted by Charles Mills in 1860. And what a lively scene that was: sailing ships and barges, animals and people; the Shannon at the height of its glory.

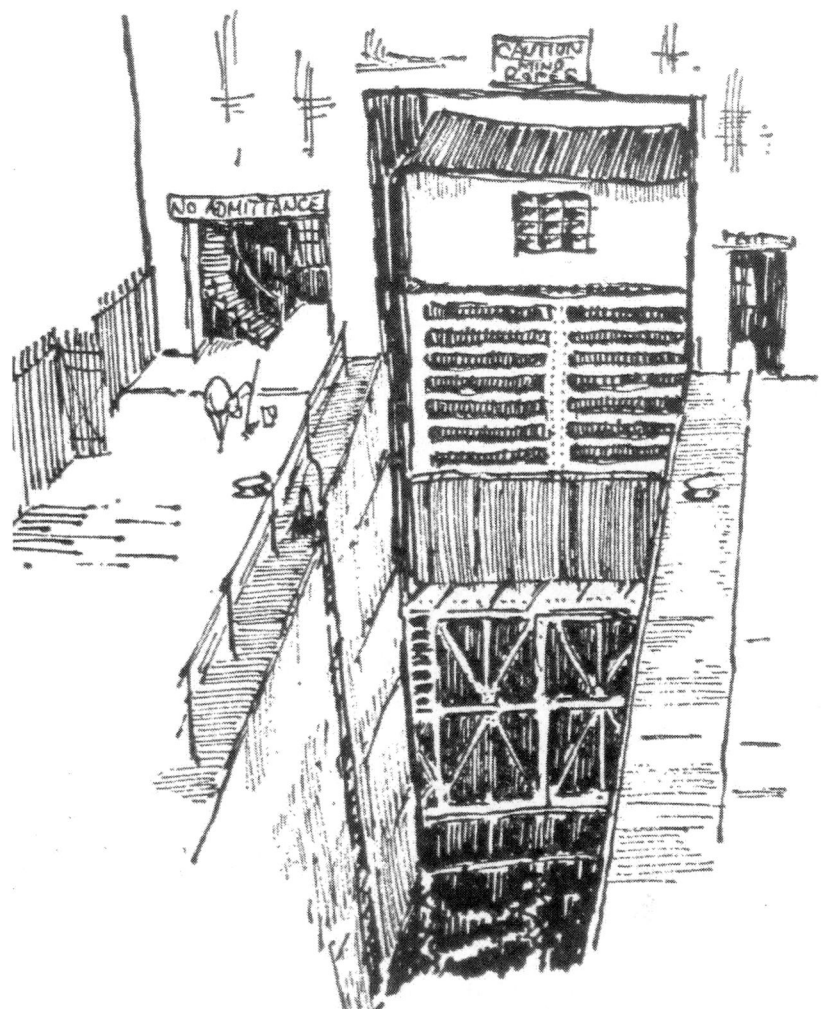

THE BARROW NAVIGATION

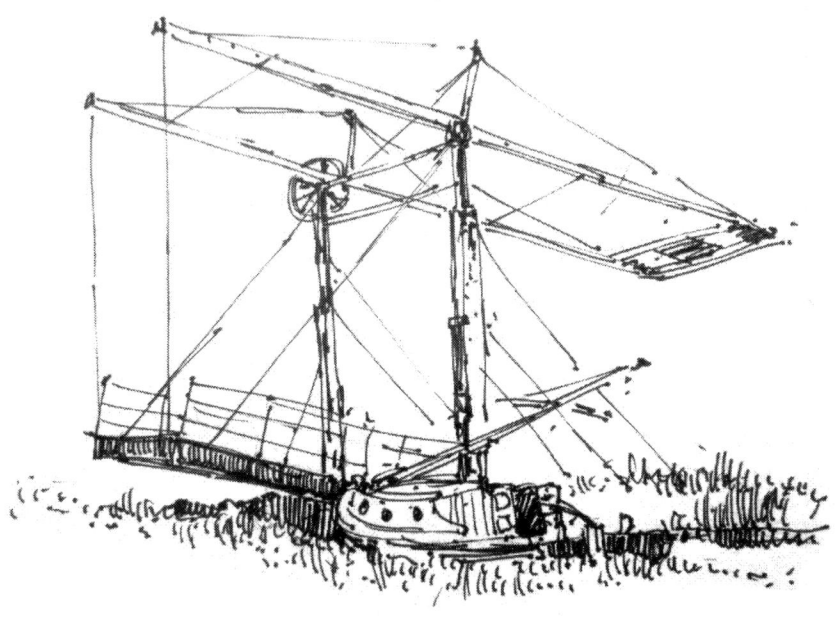

From Killaloe we returned to the Grand Canal, for the time had come for us to do battle with the Barrow Navigation. We still did not know the state of affairs with regards to navigating that elusive waterway. Was the weir still down, or had some other catastrophe befallen the waterway since our last enquiry? Even assuming that the weirs and locks were in order, would the weeds have a stranglehold on the channel? Putting together the evidence of the previous ten years it looked suspiciously as if the authorities did not want boats to pass down Barrow. It was doubtful if a pass would be granted for us to even attempt the journey. But we would soon know one way or the other, for it was at Shannon Harbour that the pass for our journey would be issued.

It was dark by the time we had moored below the locks at Shannon Harbour and rather than disturb the lock-keeper we decided to wait until morning. Perhaps after a good breakfast he would be in a mood to write a pass for wherever we should care to choose, and moreover, to do it without troubling to ask Dublin for instructions. Once we had permission for our journey in writing we felt that weedy channels and broken weirs would be minor obstacles. But even by ten o'clock the next morning James Connolly still hadn't had chance to put his teeth in. He had been up all night with a sick calf. Paper work was a nuisance at the best of times and he was grateful to see that I had already jotted down the relevant details. All he had to do was copy them into his ledger and this he proceeded to do without batting an eye.

Name of Boat: Jessica
Name of Owner: Burnett.
Journey: Shannon Harbour to St Mullins.

He tore out the yellow page that was to be our copy and wished us good luck. We shook him by the hand, cranked up the engine, and went on our way.

Four days later we tied Jessica to a bollard so weather worn and scarred by ropes that it looked like a totem pole. We were moored at the junction of the Barrow Branch of the Grand Canal. Ahead of us lay one of the least explored waterways in Europe. Its beginning is marked insignificantly by an ugly early concrete era footbridge. Beyond that a reedy channel stretched into the distance. We were somewhat relieved to observe that the reeds looked rather straggly, and between them, like a footpath through a field of hay, ran a narrow thread of clear water.

Before venturing further we went to see Ted Barrett of Joy Line Cruisers as we knew he was a campaigner for the revival of the waterway. His boatyard is situated right next to the junction of the Barrow Branch and so he is was placed to know all that goes on. At first he sounded very pessimistic about our chances but then, when he could see that we were not to be easily deterred, he warmed to the idea and thought that we should make it. He told us that one boat had managed to get up from Athy towed by a tractor and that the weir was reputed to have been repaired. He dare not allow his own boats down, other than before the weeds take hold at the very beginning of the season, for the chances are that he'd never get them back again! However, by the time we were ready to leave he was so full of enthusiasm that he decided to allow one of his boats to accompany us to Monasterevin. The family aboard were passionately keen on the Irish canals; they lived in the Channel Islands but spent their holidays on the Grand Canal and Shannon.

We set out early the next morning. Beside me in the cockpit was our bread-knife. It is an essential item for clearing weeds from the propeller, a job that I became expert at in the weeks that followed. The weeds along the Barrow, in particular the reed variety, cannot be thrown off the propeller by putting the engine into astern. Instead they have to be cut and torn away by hand. By doing an acrobatic act over the stern I could just manage to reach down to make the attack. It was not pleasant hanging upside down with my nose just a few inches from the exhaust pipe, but it was an easier way of doing the job than what the hire boat crew were faced with. The only way they could get to their propeller was to dive under the boat. I shall always remember the scene: bubbles coming up from the son down below while the father dressed in swimming trunks and a plastic mac, gamely waiting his turn on the bank.

After two miles we came to the remains of a branch canal and on investigation found that it connected with the Milltown Feeder which at this point is only a hundred yards away. Along the canal is a derelict lock. This was originally the route by which the Barrow Branch joined the Grand Canal, the junction being made immediately above the lock at Lowtown. However, subsidence of the bog was such that by 1803 the banks were down to water level. This necessitated lowering the level of that section so that the present link could make a junction with the Grand Canal, below rather than above the lock. James Goulding, who recently retired after fifty years in the Company's service, recalls that his father remembered the passage of empty boats through the old lock during the early years of his life. This was to evade the payment of tolls at Lowtown, a practice that was later prohibited.

Soon after passing the old canal cut we came to the first of the nine falling locks that lie along the 28 miles between Lowtown and Athy. Two of these locks are double and all are in good condition. They are the same size as the locks along the main line of the Grand Canal and, as on the main line, there is a good ratio of look-keepers. This was a luxury that we did not expect for the number of boats that have passed through this section in recent years can be counted on the fingers of one hand. But in the absence of length-men the work of a lock-keeper involves more than just seeing boats through locks. There are banks to be maintained and feeders and overflows to be kept clear; work that goes on day in day out, boats or no boats. Also, because canals often serve a secondary but important and lucrative function as water supply channels to the factories along their route, weed growth must be kept in check so as not to obstruct the flow. In fact, the economics are such that it is cheaper to keep a canal open than it is to keep it closed. Moreover, it is considerably cheaper to restore an abandoned waterway, than to eliminate it altogether by filling it in.

The second lock follows soon after the first and the going beyond that was much easier. It seemed almost as if the first stretch was purposely kept bad as a deterrent. For the next few miles we had a boat's width of clear water and every now and then passing places had been hacked out of the reeds. We moored for lunch in the trough of a small aqueduct. On any other canal it would have been inconsiderate of us to have blocked the channel in this way, but on the Barrow Branch it was a one chance in a thousand that another boat would want to pass by. It was as well that we stopped to fortify ourselves when we did, for around the corner the weeds were worse than ever and just below the surface was a luscious green grass. Water-lilies also grew in profusion and their stems tangled around the propeller like rope. For a mile we managed to make spasmodic progress, but then the way ahead became too much for Jessica's 4hp engine and we resorted to bow-hauling. This was not a success, for although the towpath was in excellent condition there was too great a margin of reeds between the bank and the boat. It is strange how often the condition of a towpath is inversely proportional to the condition of the canal that it serves. The towpaths of some of the busiest of all pleasure cruising waterways are impassable for much of their length, yet the towpath of the Barrow is a veritable highway. We thought that poling might be a better way of getting through the worst patches and to this end we went off with the log-saw in search of suitable saplings. After an hour of very prickly work we had two long poles; not very straight, but at least something to fight with. From the map we calculated that the third lock could not be more than half a mile away and we eventually poled up to its gates. Below the lock we were able to make headway under power again and it was not long before the town of Rathangan came into sight.

We moored for the night below the double locks at Rathangan. Before we had been there long a group of people gathered on the bridge and stared down at us, a sure indication that not many boats pass this way. We noticed that the cottage opposite took its water by the bucket full from the canal, but although the canal water appeared clean and clear we did not to risk it for drinking. Norma asked one of the onlookers how far it was to the nearest pump. The reply was a paradoxical: a quarter of a mile by bike, but half a mile if you walk! Rathangan is an attractive town and the gables, archways and colour-washed walls give it a continental feel.

Close to our mooring at Rathangan a canal milestone read: Monas Evan~/. This we translated to read: Monasteregin 4, but even taking these to be Irish miles it did not quite fit, for the distance measured from the map was at least six English miles. However, had we been asked to guess the distance after navigating it the next day I am sure that we would have come up with nothing less than ten! We had weeds all the way and one terrible stretch out in the wilds. The hire cruiser had gone on ahead and we first realised that things were getting bad when over the tops of the reeds it we sighted its coach-roof, immobile in the middle of the channel. In amongst the luxuriant growth where we both became stuck we found the remains of a wharf. Further investigation revealed the metals of a tramway that had once run to a quarry about a mile away. Most of the line had been taken up but the rails could be found serving as makeshift fences in the surrounding fields. At the wharf we unearthed a miniature turn-table - part of it was in the bottom of the canal - which had enabled the wagons to connect with two branch lines that ran along the quay. The gauge of the line was 1ft 11ins, and I later learnt that it was in use right up until the end of commercial traffic in 1959.

The second double lock is at Ballykelly, just beyond where we had been stuck. We passed through that in fine style with the lock-keeper dressed in his best bib and tucker. Alas, his rig out was not for our benefit but rather that he had just returned from an important function. But it did remind me of a directive sent out at the time of the official opening of the Grand Canal: "...for the grand tour of inspection the lock-keepers and their families to be dressed in their best apparel, their places neat and lock-houses white-washed". In any case it would have been difficult to proceed with pomp and dignity when the channel resembled a field rather than a canal. Our arrival at Monasterevin was also most unceremonious. There the channel broadens out into a thick carpet of chick-weed and thanks to an untimely air-lock in the fuel pipe Jessica drifted to a halt right in the middle of it. We both instantly bent down to prod the carburetor float needle but only succeeded in banging our heads together. Eventually the lock-keeper came and towed us in at the end of a rope.

James Moore's first job for any boat that approaches from the direction of the Grand Canal is that of bridge keeper, for at Monasterevin there is a drawbridge similar to the type found along the Llangollen Canal in Wales. The River Barrow Navigation has a number of these bridges, but none of them are balanced as well as they should be. Immediately beyond the drawbridge a magnificent aqueduct carries the canal over the River Barrow. Although the aqueduct cannot boast of any great height it is nevertheless a work of massive scale. There is a wide towpath on each side of the trough and three great limestone arches have been stained yellow where water has seeped through. It is this accidental splash of colour, together with some fine wrought iron railings, that add a master-stroke the structure. Where the trough of the aqueduct ends the branch canal to Mountmellick begins and just around the corner is the next lock. Monasterevin promised to be a capital in the world of canals and we spent the next few days moored above the lock. James Moore was pleased to have us there and no sooner had we tied up than he brought for us a present of freshly picked mushrooms.

James Moore (brother of Peter Moore, lock-keeper at Ringsend Basin, Dublin) has spent all his working life on the canals and his father before him. He started out weed cutting on the Mountmellick Branch. He and his mate did the bottom half of that canal between them. It was a distance of six miles and they were allowed three weeks for the job. They had no new-fangled machinery but used a scythe tied between two ropes. After they had finished there would not be a trace of weed. But James Moore was adamant: "The best way to get rid of weeds would be to get loaded boats back again. It was a terrible shame that they ever took them off. I missed them so much at first that I couldn't sleep at nights. It broke my heart. Then it all went downhill; I couldn't get oil for the bridge or grease for the racks. It was a twenty-four hour a day job in the early days, but I'd rather have that than fill my timesheet in for doing 'nowt, which is what I do now".

Another person who could tell me about weed cutting techniques and the day to day working of the canal was Patrick Kavanagh, retired Canal Agent for the town of Monasterevin. The Canal Agent's job was that of area manager. Even in retirement Pat Kavanagh looked every bit the part: a corpulent, waist-coated and bespectacled figure, with a trilby hat upon his head. He believed that a grab line was one of the best ways of keeping weeds down for it uprooted them, whereas the weed cutting machines of today only clip them off just below water level. And that makes them grow all the more, like pruning an apple tree. Pat Kavanagh further explained James Moore's description of a scythe between two ropes. Actually they were not regular scythes but specially made blades. As for his job as Canal Agent he told me: "I started work as a store-man in the canal depot and later they offered me the job of agent. They gave me a telephone and a bank account and that was it, I was on my own. I had to pay the wages and find the traffic. Two pounds a week was what they paid me, that and a free house". The Canal Agent was the proverbial maid of all work. He had to keep Dublin informed of movements of boats, accept and dispatch goods, keep accounts, settle disputes and solicit for cargoes.

In the 1930's the Grand Canal Company had its own fleet of motor lorries and it was the agent's job to supervise these too. Pat Kavanagh remembers that the cabs were fitted with recording discs so that a check could be kept on the length of stops. He also had to go out with the ice-breaker when it was needed. For this job they used a steam tug that normally towed chains of barges from Carlow to Athy. In Pat Kavanagh's back garden there is the remains of a double lock that dates back to the days before the aqueduct was built. Originally boats locked down to the waters of the Barrow, sailed across the river, and then climbed out again by way of a single lock at the other side. There is not much to see of the double lock for when Pat Kavanagh came to live there he dedicated himself to the task of filling it in - a long job with only a donkey and cart to fetch rubble. However, the bridge that spanned the lock chamber not only still stands, but still carries traffic. It can best be seen from the garden of the house across the road, for they have converted its arch into a garage. The design is that of a typical canal bridge with the exception that on each side of the arch there are carved recesses in the stone work. Similar recesses can be found on some of the River Barrow bridges and it is believed that they were intended to take effigies of the river gods. As for the single lock at the other side of the river, only a shallow depression in the ground indicates where this used to be.

Like Shannon Harbour, Monasterevin is a gold mine for the Industrial Archaeologist. The town owes its prosperity to the coming of the canal and a vast array of warehouses, malthouses, stables and stores have grown up beside it. The extent of these is not immediately obvious for two basins and a short arm of the canal have been filled in and buildings that once stood by the waterside now boarder onto dry land. Monasterevin's principal industries were brewing, distilling, and tobacco. But just as the rise of the town went hand in hand with the success of the canal, so its fall was linked to the canal's decline. Soon after the coming of the railway age it was said that Monasterevin is like a beauty of fifty-five with her great days behind her.

As on the main line of the Grand Canal, passenger services were also operated on the Barrow Branch and on the River Barrow Navigation. Hotels were built at Monasterevin, Carlow and Graiguenamanagh. The hotel at Monasterevin still stands and has recently been converted into flats. It is a fine Georgian building, but on a smaller, more domestic scale than its counterparts on the Grand Canal. In 1786, the year in which the canal was opened to Monasterevin, it was resolved that: "a lamp be erected at Monasterevin where the passengers land out of the Passenger Boats and that Mr. Bean be requested to provide a Globe or Lantern with six Burners to light the Passengers to and from the Boat to the Inns at Monasterevin in the mornings and evenings". In later years the hotel served as the Agent's house and Pat Kavanagh told me that in the cellar there is still the big oven in which they baked the passenger's bread.

The canal from Monasterevin to Mountmellick was abandoned in 1960. It was 11½ miles long and had a total of three locks. From the junction it is only a short walk to the first of the locks and it was there that I met John Coughlan, retired lock-keeper of Coolnaferagh. Never has history seemed further from the dull pages of text books than it did in the presence of John Coughlan. It was not that I gathered a wealth of information. John Coughlan is deaf and conversation is difficult. It was more a case of coming face to face with the living tissue of the past. Beneath the brim of a greasy old hat there is a mischievous twinkle in the eyes of John Coughlan, and the lines and the whiskers on his face frequently screw up into a grin that reveals crooked brown teeth. His left hand remains permanently cupped to his ear, while his right clutches a stick. The stick is not so much for leaning on as for waving about in the air to add physical force to the words he speaks. His every statement is prefixed with "Do you know!" "Do you know, five generations of Coughlans have grown up in that house! Do you know, my great grandfather worked the Tullamore to Dublin mail packet boat! Do you know, it was slave labour in those days, but there was something in it that kept you at it! Do you know, I had a chair outside in summer and I'd sit there from ten at night to five in the morning and in that time see five or six boats through!"

I hired a bicycle to explore the Mountmellick Canal. Beyond the first lock the channel has been drained and the towpath is overgrown. This, together with the skeletons of the lock gates, gives the impression that the canal has been abandoned for a hundred years, rather than just over ten. The canal meanders through open countryside along a route that called for no remarkable feat of engineering. It must have been a wonderful waterway to navigate, for the Slieve Bloom Mountains are a back-drop to every vista. The canal passes through the town of Portarlington. At this point a by-pass has been made along the bed of the canal and the lock cottage now looks out onto a stretch of tarmac. But the saddest sight of all is the canal terminal at Mountmellick. This fine basin, with its warehouses and stores, is now ignominiously used as the town's rubbish dump.

While rummaging in the remains of Mountmellick's canal basin I was harassed by tinkers. Irish tinkers can be brazen beggars who wear their quarry down by persistently nagging for "pence". Later I came upon their camp and learnt a little of their way of life. Unlike the gypsies of England, the Irish tinkers have not deserted their traditional wagons and horse dealings in favour of motor vans and scrap metal. It is said that the majority of the horses in Ireland are in the hands of the tinker community and canvas topped wagons are a familiar sight along the roadsides. Many of the wagons have been let go, but the best are kept clean and gaily painted. It was the Touhy's that I spoke to and they told me that there is a man living in Birr who can still make you a wagon. He can decorate it too and it will cost about £300. In the files of Irish bureaucracy the tinker community comes under the heading of itinerates and efforts are being made to squash their nomadic way of life and neatly settle them in permanent sites. In the words of the folk song made famous by the Dubliners:

> *Goodbye to the tent and the old caravan,*
> *To the tinker, the rover, the travelling man...*
> *There's a bylaw to say you must be on your way*
> *And another to say you can't wander.*

On my return to Jessica that evening I was just in time to see maintenance boat 90E nosing her way into the lock. She had come up from Athy, news which we greeted with jubilation for it meant a relatively clear channel. We watched her rise slowly in the lock and then, with the engine in ahead, gently push open the top gates. The crew told us that their next job was to repair the first bridge on the Mountmellick Canal. The bridge is no more than 50 yards from the junction but it took them an hour to reach it.

At this point there is a page missing from my original manuscript. But as the proceeding page ends with the words: "weeds were the height of a man and in a number of places we saw them being cut for thatch" I can all too well recollect the contents. Weeds were so thick that the canal and a field on the opposite side to the towpath became indistinguishable from each other. A herd of cattle grazing in the field had likewise ceased to tell the difference for as we attempted to bow haul Jessica they waded right alongside. Cows we could cope with but amongst them were a couple of ferocious bulls. Rather than risk being attacked on water I jumped ship and towed her until a barbed wire fence put us out of danger. Shortly afterwards we passed over a small aqueduct and found upon it a moss encrusted plague that read: Gratton Aqueduct, Richard EVans, Engineer, 1790. But cattle apart, the most remarkable sight that morning was a boat for ferrying from one side of the canal to the other. It was built entirely of corrugated iron!

By early afternoon we were moored at Vicarstown, the half way point along the level to Athy. Vicarstown has a range of canal buildings out of all proportion to its size and population, but which can be explained by the fact that its wharf also served the neighbouring town of Stradbally. The canal traveler would be well advised to walk the three miles to Stradbally for the Irish Steam Preservation Society has a museum there. Or better still, if the stay at Vicarstown can be timed to tie in with the August Bank Holiday weekend, a visit can be made to the Society's annual rally. Traction engine enthusiasts from all over Ireland bring their machines to the event. There are also steam trains, threshing machines, a fairground organ, vintage cars and motorbikes.

The only difficulty that we encountered along the remainder of the level to Athy was a floating Sargasso Sea of weed that had been churned up by the propeller of 90E. A particularly bad stretch of this weed had accumulated above the lock and we had to bow haul Jessica for the last few hundred yards. There are three locks at Athy and the canal between them contained the only dirty water that we encountered in Ireland. A black fermenting scum bubbled on the surface and old prams and bicycles lurked in the depths. To add to this we were followed by a horde of children. Their faces gleamed down on us from each bridge parapet and as we passed beneath their range we braced ourselves, just as canal travelers in Birmingham, Liverpool and Manchester instinctively brace themselves at each bridge hole in anticipation of a globule of spit or a carefully aimed half brick. But dirty water and troublesome children aside, the Athy canalside is distinguished by a fine row of cottages and the town it has an 18th century Court House and marketplace. A more recent Dominican church is a dominant feature of Athy. It has a hyperbolic paraboloid roof: an architectural feature for which the 20th century is likely to be best remembered by.

Below the bottom lock the still water canal ends and the River Barrow Navigation begins. Navigation on the Barrow goes back to medieval times. In 1531 an Act was passed by the Irish parliament titled, "An Act for the Weares upon the Barrow, and other waters in the county of Kilkenny". It mentions that from time immemorial "boates, scowts, wherries, clarans, cottes, and other vessels" had been navigating the waters of the Barrow. The Act went on to state that the owners of mill-ponds were to leave a sufficient gap in their weirs to allow the free passage of vessels, and that seven feet of plain ground be allowed for a towing path. But it was not until 1751 that any substantial progress was made towards improving the waterway for regular trade. In that year the Commissioners of Ireland Navigation were established and they granted £2,000 to remove obstructions between Monasterevin and St Mullins. The engineer in charge was Thomas Omer. For the next 40 years work was sporadically carried out, but by 1790 only seven locks had been built and it was reported that 18 tons was the largest capacity boat that could ply upon the river during the summer months. Thirty years later the river was still said to be unsatisfactory and it was not until 1838 that worthwhile tonnages could be carried. But the Barrow, with floods on the one hand and droughts on the other, was never an entirely satisfactory waterway, which is frequently the case with river navigations. It is interesting to note that in 1812 a plan was proposed for a still water canal from Athy to Kilkenny. This would have followed a 200 foot contour and locks were not considered necessary throughout its 24 miles. The scheme was put forward by the citizens of Kilkenny but opposed by the Barrow Navigation Company.

As Jessica emerged from the bottom lock at Athy her engine faltered; it was as if for one moment she had second thoughts about going through with what lay ahead. Fortunately it soon picked up again for immediately beyond the lock the Barrow tumbles over a weir and it is necessary to pass close to the edge in order to enter the canal cut. This is a fitting beginning for a waterway that has always been considered hazardous to navigate. In the days of commercial carrying such difficulties demanded a special breed of boatmen. The distance between Athy and St Mullins is 41 miles and there are 23 locks, one of which is a double one. The approach to the locks is by way of side canals, and these cuttings vary in length from a few yards to more than two miles.

The first of these canal cuts leads to Ardreigh Lock. There is a drawbridge along this stretch of canal that is left open and this, together with an absence of weeds, gave us a clear run through. Although Athy is only a short walk away, Ardreigh Lock is deep in the countryside and an ideal mooring place. It was from there that I visited the museum at Robertstown. The word "ATHY" drawn in large letters on the back of my map as a plea to passing motorists, reminds me that I hitch-hiked there and back!

We continued our journey down the Barrow in the warmth of a summer's day. Ahead of us simmered a hazy landscape of meadows, trees and placid water. Under such ideal conditions we were tempted to dash on down the river before something happened to spoil it all; before it dried up or flooded, or before the weirs collapsed and the locks crumbled.

On the river stretches we steered so as to keep ten or fifteen feet from the towpath side, for it is there that the dredged channel is reputed to be. It is necessary to keep a careful lookout for the canal cuts for they can easily slip by unnoticed. Frequently they show up just at the last minute above the weir. When that happens the weir is usually constructed in such a way that it skirts the navigable channel up to the entrance of the canal cut. Thus, one is precariously steering between the bank and the edge of the weir for a distance of fifty yards or so. With the exception of Carlow, none of the weirs are guarded, as they are on the Thames for instance, and if there is any amount of flood water in the river I can imagine that the approaches could be very difficult to negotiate. At the time of our voyage there was no large scale chart published that indicated exactly what the layout was at the entrance to each canal and the uncertainty of what came next was one of our biggest problems. Since our journey, the Carlow Branch of the Inland Waterways Association of Ireland has produced an excellent guide to the river. But perhaps the best and most interesting guide, not only to the Barrow but to all of Ireland's waterways, would be a strip map compiled from facsimiles of the early 6in Ordnance Survey. These sheets, which date from the middle of the 19th century, contain a wealth of detail and are in effect an historical document.

After two miles of river a canal leads to Levitstovrn Lock. This is the longest canal cut and along it there is a curious lift bridge. Instead of being hinged drawbridge fashion the span remains horizontal and is hoisted vertically to give headroom. But the most bizarre feature of its design is the relationship of its moving parts: where one stands to crank the handle corresponds exactly to the fall of the counterbalance weight. Consequently, an unsuspecting operator can merrily lower two tons of cast iron right down upon his head! There is a cottage close to the bridge and there I met John Dooley who has spent a lifetime working on the Barrow, much of it aboard a steam dredger. "She wouldn't do a thing unless the pressure was above 80lbs, not even lift an empty bucket. But that was the best way to dredge as It didn't damage the bed of the canal, not like a drag-line dredger". He showed me a flat bottomed boat that was tied up at the side of the canal. Her sides were of heavy clinker laid planks and both bow and stern came to a point so that there was no means of differentiating between the two. John Dooley told me that she had been built to carry the material used to construct the mill by the lock. If this is so the boat would be in the region of hundred years old and very likely a surviving example of the type of craft that navigated the Barrow in the days before Grand Canal barges. In 1821 it was stated that trade was carried in light vessels carrying about 10 tons each and drawing about eighteen inches of water. The mill by the lock was the first of several that we were to see on the Barrow, all built during the hey-day of trade and since fallen into disuse. It is a huge seven story building with mock battlements along the roof parapets.

In the eight miles between Levitstown and Carlow there are only two locks, Mageney and Bestfield. The cuts leading to both of these are only a matter of a hundred yards long but badly silted. Even Jessica with her mere eighteen inches of draught was stirring up the bottom, and at Bestfield she actually went aground. The lock gates creaked and groaned in protest as we passed through. At Mageney the deserted lock-house had grass growing from the top of its chimney. The river stretches also seemed shallow in places and at times we had to steer a crooked course to dodged great clumps of reeds. Above Carlow it is a dark, brooding river, a macabre river that carried the carcass of a cow in its stream.

The entry to Carlow is heralded by the chimney and pipe lines of the sugar factory. Some suddenly roar out clouds of steam that makes you jump, others bubble away contentedly. The navigable arch beneath Carlow Bridge is on extreme left. It is the last one that you see when coming downstream and the most unlikely one of them all. The arch is marked by red and black blobs of paint. Below the bridge a long weir sweeps across the river and the lock is at the extreme right-hand side of this. The lock-keeper sat dozing in a chair and only stirred to inspect our pass. Below the lock the way was blocked by two maintenance boats, but as we did not intend going further that day we tied up astern of them.

We had not been at Carlow long before Bob Shirley, Barrow

enthusiast extraordinary, came to see us. In a hushed voice he told us the lament of the river since the days of commercial carrying. It was a tale of many set-backs and few boats. During each of the previous three seasons there had always been something somewhere along the line to effectively stop navigation. He was critical about the day to day maintenance of the waterway: those who work on the river spend most of their time drinking tea. It was a feeling echoed by others too. Indeed, during the two days that we spent at Carlow the crew of the maintenance boats did absolutely nothing at all. They just sat in the sun yawning. Before he left Bob Shirley filled half a note book with hints on the route that lay ahead of us.

Carlow neglects its river frontage, which is unfortunate for it has the potentially of being the most beautiful part of the town. Beyond the top gates of the lock a long low round-topped wall divides the road from the river. It dates from an age when stone was abundant and men had an instinctive sense of proportion. Towering above it is the silo of an animal feed factory. Not knowing what I was letting myself in for, I asked if I might go to the top of the silo to take a photograph. After agreeing that it would be entirely at my own risk I was loaded onto a vertical conveyor belt. The arrangement was such that I had just a hand and a foot hold, and in this precarious fashion I ascended. For a view of Carlow, the top of the silo cannot be bettered and the ascent has the making of a tourist attraction. I learnt that the factory uses the waters of the Barrow to drive a turbine, the race for which runs beside the lock.

At Carlow the Barrow Navigation changes character. Above the town the going is reasonably easy but the landscape cannot be said to be anything exceptional. Below Carlow it is the reverse: the scenery improves but the navigation deteriorates. Throughout the navigation's history Carlow has always been the dividing point between passable and impassable; 50 ton loads and 30 ton loads; trade and no trade.

Along the two miles below Carlow Lock this change became apparent. The river flowed faster and the reeds grew thicker. We passed straggling islands of reeds and just beneath the surface we could see a continual cover of green stems, all bowing and waving in the direction of the flow. The canal to Clogrennan Lock is pointed out by a makeshift signpost, which is just as well for you might otherwise never believe that it could be a canal. It is a narrow channel camouflaged by the boughs of overhanging trees. The lock was also more decrepit than its predecessors. The gates were difficult to open and when I lifted the paddles clouds of muddy water billowed away downstream. There is very little fall for Clogrennan Lock was an afterthought, an improvement made 40 years after the rest. On the credit side it was along the two miles below Carlow that we caught our first faint blue glimpse of the hills that lay ahead.

In contrast to the diminutive beginnings of Clogrennan Cut, the entrance to the canal at Milford is so wide that we entered it without knowing. We had been following Bob Shirley's instructions to keep close to the west bank. This we did until we ran into a vast swamp of tangled weeds. Thinking that this could not be right, we began to pole Jessica out again but then noticed a quay wall and the canal towpath. It was an excellent towpath and from it we bow-hauled Jessica the half mile or so to the lock.

Bob Shirley's notes never painted things as black as they are. They had been given in a spirit of encouragement. It is a way with the Irish. When we came to bits that said bad or very bad, and had twirls of scribble to denote weeds, we dare not imagine what we might be in for. One such place was the weir at Rathvindon. Perhaps it was because the three miles of river below Milford had been something of an improvement that the sudden barrage of weed at Rathellen seemed all the worse. The only possible way of entering the canal was by finding the clearer water at the very edge of the weir. There was not much flow on the river and had we have been confident that there was no underwater obstructions we could have tackled this quite easily by approaching at full speed. By this means Jessica would have had enough way on her to drift through no matter how tangled her propeller came. But we dare not do that. Instead we erred on the side of caution and came into the bank long beforehand. For the next hour we bow hauled and poled and generally thrashed out a channel towards the lock. As a consolation we found the remains of an apple orchard on Company ground and decided that we had earned at least a sack full.

We moored for the night above Rathvindon Lock and spent the evening inspecting the river down to Leighlinbridge. It was weedy, but as it had a noticeable flow we decided that, at the worst, we could drift down. The lock-house at Rathvindon was being converted into a week-end cottage, the first such conversion we had seen in Ireland. Along the canals in England this has become the trend and any waterside property is now worth a pot of gold. But in Ireland empty lock-cottages, warehouses and stores go a begging.

The next lock below Rathvindon is Rathellen. A canal over a mile long leads to this lock and since the beginning of my account of the Barrow I have been carefully saving up adjectives in order to do it justice. If you can recall the classic film African Queen you will be able to conjure up the condition of the Rathellen canal, for I believe that some of the scenes must surely have been shot there on location. At first we did not credit that it could be true. We had got to where we knew the canal should branch off but all that there appeared before us were green fields. Slowly it dawned upon us that one of those fields, the long narrow one, was in fact the canal! We drifted gingerly up to the edge of this field and sure enough, beneath that jungle of vegetation there was water. By using the dinghy as a sort of stepping stone we managed to get ashore. At least we presumed that it was the shore, for although visually there was no difference our feet did not get wet. The next two hours were spent bow-hauling Jessica at a snail's pace towards the look. After the first few hundred yards the channel improved a little but the towpath got worse. We plodded through high nettles and got caught up in barbed wire fences. One would think that the least the Barrow maintenance crew could do is clear a decent towpath.

Below Rathellen Lock the Barrow, as if anxious to make amends, is wide and clear. It is indeed fitting that the river should pull itself together and take on a more stately appearance for ahead of us was the grandiose town of Muine Bheag. On approaching from the river it is the imposing Doric portico of the Court House that first gives an indication that this is no ordinary town. Muine Bheag was founded towards the end of the 18th century by Walter Bagenal and he intended it to be of considerable architectural pretense and to bear the name of Versailles. Alas the re-routing of the coach road put pay to Walter's ambitions and left the town with no prouder title than Bagenalstown, a name that it kept until the 20th century. But what poor Walter could not foresee was that in less than a hundred years warehouses, mills, malthouses and workshops would be built on the sight of his fairy tale city. Moreover, they would be built by men who had never heard of Doric porticos. Theirs was an entirely different kind of architecture, but a kind which nevertheless produced fine functional buildings that are worth a dozen Greek or Roman façades.

Bagenalstown became an important station on the Barrow Navigation. Considerable wheat was shipped from there and in addition to brewing the town had two mills. The quaysides alongside the canal are a testimony to this trade. It begins with a superb malt house and ends with the extensive Lodge Mills. The lock takes its name from these mills and above it a monstrous steel girder drawbridge spans the canal. The bridge is so badly balanced that not even the pull of two adults on its chain could begin to lift it. Fortunately Jessica's passage through the town had attracted a score of onlookers and their additional bulk made up for so many deficient hundredweights of counterbalance.

As we worked through the lock the children that Jessica had pipe-piped along with her either pushed the wrong way on the balance beams or just stood and gaped. It seemed that a generation is growing up on the banks of the Barrow that has never seen the mechanics of the navigation work. Lodge Lock has a fall of ten feet and is the deepest on the waterway.

We moored that night to a pleasant grassy bank just below the lock gates. Downstream a narrow bank separates the navigable channel from the main course of the river. But the bank does not entirely keep the force of the river at bay for in places it spills over and there is a fast flow. While I was wondering how a loaded barge could have made headway against the current I noticed, in the long grass beside the towpath, the rusty remains of winches and cables. During the 1930's a drainage scheme caused the quick run-off of water from the upper reaches of the river and this aggravated the difficulties of maintaining the navigation. The Grand Canal Company received compensation and in an attempt to retain a regular service south of Carlow installed over seventy winches. These were positioned at strategic points and from them ran cables of up to 500 yards long. Above Carlow the Company placed an 80hp tug on the river to assist barges during the winter floods. The attempt is reminiscent of those made on other fast flowing rivers and in particular, along the River Rhone in France.

Along the six miles between Bagenalstown and Goresbridge there are three locks: Fenniscourt, Sliguff, and Upper Ballyellen.

There is a lock-keeper at Fenniscourt and everything about the lock is kept in such good trim that one might suspect that it had been transplanted from the Thames. Sliguff is the opposite. The approach is weedy and the lock-house was all boarded up. On the river below Sliguff we had more weeds and this time they were so bad that we had to drift and paddle our way to Upper Ballyellen. It was the weir at Upper Ballyellen that had caused the stoppage for most of that year. When we passed one of the maintenance boats was moored across it. A great deal of mystery surrounds the weir at Upper Ballyellen. Officially it was washed away by the winter floods but for anyone who cares to keep an ear to the ground there are tales of a blast of dynamite. Perhaps the blast shook the timbers of Upper Ballyellen Lock, for it was in a most decrepit state. Almost as much water leaked out through the bottom gates as what came in through the fully open paddles of the top gate.

The next morning we were despondent as we made ready to tackle another day's journey. Our voyage through that dilapidated waterway was beginning to wear us down. Even Diana, whose job it was each morning to pump the bilge, no longer tackled the task with the same gusto. But the Barrow has a way of rewarding her devotees and at that moment of despair two small cabin cruisers rounded the bend of the canal. We had not seen a pleasure boat for over two weeks and we could not have been more surprised had two crocodiles swum up to the lock. Pat and Anna, Noel, Paddy, and dog, had sailed from Dublin. They always spent their holidays on the Grand Canal or Shannon but this was the first time they had tried the Barrow. Along the way they had encountered the same hardships that we had and more besides. On the first day of their holiday one of the boats sank from under them. Undaunted they raised it up again and put the bunk cushions through a mangle. Their struggles with the Barrow had left them so weary and bemused that on one occasion they filled and emptied a lock without remembering to put the boats in! For the remainder of our journey down the Barrow the hilarious company of our fellow voyagers was never very far away.

At Goresbridge the worst of the Barrow was behind us. Below that town the river flows remarkably clear and high hills begin to pile up for a grand finale. Huge boulders begin to appear above water level, but these are well clear of the navigable channel, still fifteen feet from the towpath side. At Ballytiglea a commune of hippies had settled in the abandoned lock house and they came out to help us through. The attractive scantily clad girls among them would have walked away with any "Lock-keeper of the Year Award" and their presence might be one way of attracting boats to the Barrow.

Mr. & Mrs. Moran who live at Borris Lock are a cultural world apart, but equally as colourful. Tom Moran has worked that lock for fifty years and his wife's family worked it before him for as far back as they can remember. He told me that it had been a bad year for weed because there had not been a May flood and the roots had got a stronger hold than usual. "But there was never any weed when the barges were working. The towpath was clear too; nothing on it but horse muck". I noticed that the ground floor of their house had been filled in and that they lived upstairs. This he told me was a precaution against floods. "The worse flood was in 1947 and it started on St Patrick's Day. We were upstairs on the top of a table and it took three months to get the house clean and dry afterwards. A barge moored above the lock finished up on the towpath. In the days when we used horses they'd often have to couple up six or eight boats together and tow them up with a tug in a strong flow".

To get to Tom Moran's house you must either walk along the towpath or pass through the grounds of Borris House, seat of the Mac Murrough Kavanagh family, descendants of the kings of Leinster. A remarkable 19th century member of the family was

Arthur Mac Murrough Kavanagh who, though born severely crippled, learned not only to ride and shoot but also travelled the world and became a Member of Parliament. His grave is close to the riverside and on the day we passed two of the gardeners had been sent down to tidy it up. We found them sat on the grave stone having their lunch break, their hats hooked on top of the cross. "God rest him", they said.

From Borris the Barrow drops down to Graiguenamanagh by way of Ballingrane, Clashganny, and Ballykeenan. Ballingrane Lock is a perfect place for swimming. The water above its top gates is deep and clear and bordered by a grassy bank. At Clashganny the lock-keeper still observes the ritual of leaving the lock ready for downstream traffic even though more than ten years had passed since the last barge shot in from the weir. Ballykeenan is the double lock but its total fall is not much more than that of the single lock at Bagenalstown. A broad towpath follows the navigation and the route from Borris is through a deep wooded gorge. The town of Graiguenamanagh lies between Brandon Hill and the Blackstairs Mountains. Throughout the whole of Europe there can be few more magnificent places accessible by boat.

The quay above Graiguenamanagh Lock became almost a permanent mooring place for Jessica. Each morning the lock-keeper's wife brought us milk and fresh eggs and the town's bakery was right there on the canal side. The three bakers had recently settled an industrial dispute in a unique way. Not very long ago they had all worked for a tyrannical boss who refused to give them a rise. But rather than go on strike for better pay and conditions they simply left him and set up on their own account. Their business flourished and now if their ex-boss wants to buy bread he must buy it from them!

While at Graiguenamanagh we learnt of a survey that was being made of the Barrow Navigation by the Board of Works. It is visualised that by the mid 1970's all waterways in Ireland will have passed into the control of their department. This is welcomed news to the canal enthusiast for it is the Board of Works that is making such an excellent job of the Shannon Navigation. Later we met the survey team and learnt that this was a preliminary investigation to ascertain what exactly they would be taking on. It was to determine if, after ten years of neglect, the Barrow was worth taking on at all. I am pleased to say that the eventual decision was to retain the navigation and as I write new lock gates are being fitted, channels are being dredged, and weeds are being cleared. There is however a huge backlog of work and it will be many years hence before the Barrow is completely trouble free. But providing its future is secure I am in no hurry for that day to come. Indeed, I believe that there is an opportunity, and an argument in favour, for retaining three distinct categories of waterways in Ireland. There would be the Shannon for the sleek cruisers, the Grand Canal for quite travel, and the Barrow for adventure.

Buoyed up with the knowledge of a new lease of life for the Barrow we set sail along the last few miles. Tinnahinch Lock is a deep one and the canal that leads to it was silted and weedy when we passed, but very likely it is deep and clear by now. It is likely too that the rotten and grass grown gates of Carricklead Lock, gates that seemed to be held together only by force of habit, have been replaced by new ones. St Mullins Lock is more substantial for it keeps the tide at bay. Jessica approached It with a hint of pride. She was the first boat in four years to pass right through the Barrow Navigation.

THE RIVER NORE NAVIGATION

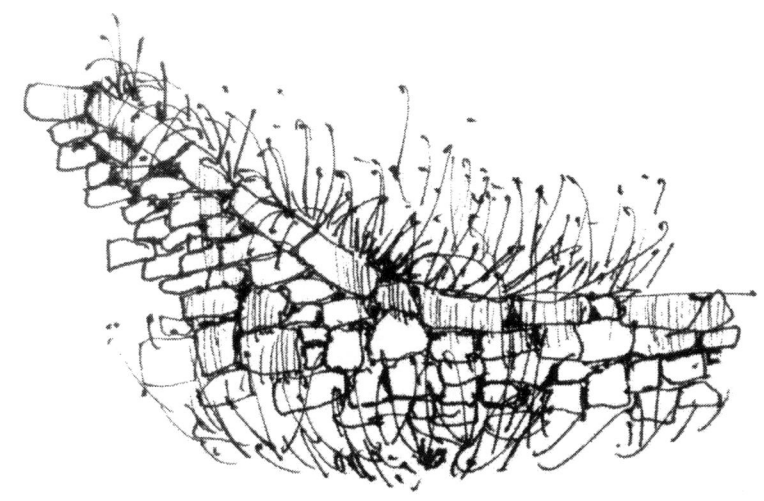

It will be remembered that, as an alternative to the Barrow Navigation, a plan was put forward for a canal from Athy to Kilkenny. Had that project come to fruition it might have given impetus for the completion of a grand scheme to link Kilkenny to the sea. The River Nore Navigation is a unique and mysterious waterway. Although at the time of our voyage its background history had been recorded in Ruth Delany's *The Canals of the South of Ireland*, little attempt had been made to systematically trace and record its features on the ground and to fit the scheme into the chronology of canal development in general. This was the task that I set myself during our stay at Graiguenarnanagh, and continued a year later when my studio was located close to the river near Inistioge.

Like the Barrow, the Nore had been navigated by small boats from early times. In 1581 it was recorded that a sum of £108

68s 8d was to be paid for a section of the river be "made passable fit and serviceable for boats of the full lading of one toun weight at all times in somer and in winter." The tide flows as far as Inistioge and with a spring rise of 15 feet it is likely that the river up to there had always been accessible to coasting vessels. Up to the early years of this century schooners loaded timber from a wharf a short distance below the town. But it was not until 1755 that work was begun in earnest on making navigable the 20 miles between Inistioge and Kilkenny. The engineer in charge was Thomas Omer. At the same time he was involved with the Shannon Navigation and Grand Canal. By 1759 it was reported that four miles of canal and 12 locks had been completed, but that was virtually as far as the work ever progressed and it as to remain as "incomplete and as useless as if it had never been begun".

The most amazing thing about the waterway is the scale upon which it was constructed. The locks measured 200ft by 14ft. It is however possible to find their likeness elsewhere. Omer himself was responsible for three early locks on the Grand Ganal which measured 136ft long, whilst contemporary locks on the rivers Hey and Kennet in England could accommodate craft 122ft by 19 ft. It must be remembered that the development of still water canals took place at a later date than the period we are considering and therefore Omer would have based his work upon established river navigations.

An important document in the study of the Nore Navigation is an illustrated map which accompanied a Parliamentary Report of 1761. The map records the works already completed and while allowance must be made for artistic license, it can be assumed that the drawings are based on fact. Details of particular interest are: decorative stone work at each side of the lock gates and the depiction of a motley collection of rowed craft and quasi Viking ships, rather than conventional barges.

An account of the money spent upon the navigation is also of interest:

20 shovel handles @ 3d......................	5s 0d
6 spade handles @ 6d........................	3s 0d
For 18 rammers.. ..	16s 8d
For 10 iron Crows, weight 3cwt lqr 141bs	£3 12s 4d
2 Hour Glasses...........................	2s 2d
11 Crows @ 8d..	7s 4d
To horse hire to Desort wood............	4s 4d
To Mr William Wilkinson for 360 elms @ 3d.....	£4 10s 0d
For 25 hand barrows @ ls 4d.......................	£ 1 13s 4d
To carriage of 14 tons, 14ft of timber.............	£ 2 17s 2d
To two barrels of grass seed to sow the banks of the canal...	£1 7s 0d
To Messrs Howard & Merry, Ship Carpenters.	£ 4 11s 0d
To expenses in launching boats...................	5s 5d

But what captured my curiosity most of all is the story of a strange deceit whereby in order to qualify for a Government Grant towards the completion of the work, a boat was manhandled over the incomplete navigation. The ruling was that the money would be paid as soon as a loaded boat could be drawn from Thomastovm to Bennettsbridge. At the time of the deceit the canal cut at Bennettsbridge did not contain water and the river between there and Thomastown was unimproved. However, according to tradition, a boat loaded with a cargo of skins was drawn up the river and dragged through the excavation made for the canal.

Perhaps to lend credibility to the deceit, in March 1761 the following report appeared in The Universal Advertiser:

Yesterday arrived here for the first time, to the great joy and satisfaction of the inhabitants of this city, three large lighters to take in goods for Waterford, which were this day laden with tallow, butter, and marble for exportation; they sailed up and down our new canal, thro' all the locks, gates, etc. with the greatest ease and safety. It is with pleasure that we see this great work, begun but three years ago, already become of real use to the public, and will speedily be, when finished, a most useful navigation.

I began my investigations at Kilkenny where the river flows beneath the walls of the castle and is bordered by an embankment known as Canal Walk. In the 1761 report this was described as "a very convenient quay, with all its slips and landing places, 300ft in length and 80ft in breadth". Over the years it has been altered and no trace of bollards or the like can be found. However, following the walk downstream one soon comes to a cutting and the remains of the first lock.

The specification for Scot's Lock is recorded in contemporary documents as follows:

Stone and other materials for building this first lock, upon the following terms, viz: hewn stone raised and cut, the faces to be punched, and the beds and ends wrought true to the square, and chiseled six inches in from the face, delivered at the lock where they are to be used and set, and a skillful person to set the said hewn stones...rough stone for building the backing of the lock and for raising the carriage to the lock...roche lime at eight pence per barrel, to be measured at the kiln and delivered to the works.

The upper gate masonry of Scot's Lock still stands as true as the day it was built. The hollow quoins to which the heel posts of the gates fitted, can be clearly seen and along the edge of the coping stones is carved the same inset convex radius that we last saw on Omer's lock at Limerick. The 1761 map shows steps and ornate scroll buttresses as part of the lock masonry, but these were not to be found, either at Scot's Look or any other upon the navigation. There is no trace of the bottom gate masonry at Scot's Lock. But this is perhaps not surprising as all the locks on the Nore Navigation were turf sided and therefore top and bottom gate masonry was not linked. Possibly the only reason why the top gate masonry of Scot's Lock has survived to this day is because a bridge which spans the chamber uses the lock walls as its abutments. A stream still runs through the cutting.

Beyond the lock a culvert enabled a brook to pass beneath the canal. According to contemporary documents this structure was completed but no trace of it remains. From the lock the line of the canal continues as a broad shallow depression and its bed was once used by the troops as a parade ground. The base of a bandstand is a reminder of those days. The towpath is bordered by huge elm trees, doubtless the ones supplied by William Wilkinson at 3d each. After a mile a bridge spans the navigation, the arch of which follows the conventional canal style. The width of the arch is what one would expect for the purpose of navigation, but the enigma is that the structure is set altogether too low down. Perhaps it has been rebuilt at this level at a later date. Shortly after the bridge is the site of the second lock.

Crow's Well Lock has survived best of all. It is located alongside the river, a situation that could account for its state of preservation. On the river side of the lock both top and bottom gate walls are intact, while on the land side they have virtually disappeared. The most likely explanation, which follows for all the locks, is that unless there was a good reason for leaving the stones in situ (e.g. bridge abutments or bank support) they were plundered and used elsewhere. It is therefore possible that some of the more embellished stone work, so far unaccounted for, may one day turn up in the walls of a house or outbuilding. Due to the sighting of Craw's Well Lock its chamber differs from the rest in that there is a stone wall between the top and bottom gates on the river side. On the land side there is the usual sloping turf wall. Its size roughly corresponds to the dimensions given in contemporary documents, i.e. 200ft by 21ft.

It might be thought safe to assume that the locks would have been built to the dimensions laid down at the time but thanks to the determined pacing of my friend Geoff Wheat it was found that the next lock was in fact only 134 feet long. This was the lock at Archerstown, and was the last on the canal from Kilkenny. At each of the gate abutments only the backing rubble remained. Soon after the lock the canal enters the river.

According to the 1761 map the navigation left the river again after only a few hundred yards. Rimer Lock was possibly a single set of flood gates, but no trace remains as the land upon which it stood has since been reclaimed and ploughed over. However, the far end of the canal shows up by the old mill at Highrath. The old 6 inch Ordnance Survey map shows an avenue of trees that is marked "Old Canal". After Highrath the navigation joins the river again until Kilferagh.

In the grounds of Kilferagh House are the remains of a two rise lock. Not only is Kilferagh Lock unique in the scale to which it was constructed but also because it appears to mark the origin of the 'double' or 'staircase' lock in this part of the world. Previously this distinction has been attributed to Henry Berry who built a two rise lock on England's St Helens Canal in 1760. However, on the Continent waterways had reached a more developed state, and one wonders if Thomas Omer had at some time come under the influence of his European counterparts. To some extent the size and styling of his work tends to bear this out.

As the locks at Kilferagh stand in private grounds I had cherished the hope that I might find them intact. But this was not so. Most of the cut stone has been removed from the sight and generally the remains are in disarray. However all three sets of gate walls are visible and the remaining masonry displays a sloping upstream edge to the abutments, a characteristic shown in the 1761 map illustrations. The canal joins the river almost immediately beyond the top and bottom gates. To warrant the fall of a double lock I would have expected considerable rapids at this point and a long cutting to by-pass them. The absence of both is yet another unresolved mystery of the Nore Navigation. The owners of Kilferagh House tell me that they have found a different strain of grass growing around the lock side. Could this have been sown from the two barrels of seed listed in the accounts?

It is difficult to determine the fall of the locks along the navigation. Figures are given in contemporary reports, although not I believe in the conventional sense. For example, Crow's Well Lock is given as 10 feet and Kilferagh a combined fall of 13 feet. But it is difficult to see how these measurements could refer to a difference in water level. More likely it means the actual height of the lock walls, or possibly the height from the base of the chamber to the water level above. With that theory, the measurements correspond closer with what can be seen on the ground. A dimension that remains unknown is the depth of water over the lock sills, and hence the maximum draught that can be accommodated.

It is interesting to speculate on the type of craft that Omer had in mind. As I have mentioned, the 1761 artist's impression shows an odd collection of vessels. Perhaps these were just figments of imagination; a decoration rather than a statement of fact. In the case of the Grand Canal it is recorded that Omer built 136ft locks with 115 ton barges in mind. Large locks for large craft! For the Nore it is possible that he also had large vessels in mind, but this time on the lines of a raft that could carry a worthwhile tonnage without having too deep a draught when it came to negotiating the shallow river stretches. Alternatively, he may have intended the locks to take a string of small boats in tow, similar to the "Tom Puddings" that in more recent times plied the Aire and Calder Navigation in England. A point that has a bearing on this theory is the relatively narrow gauge to which the bridge arches were constructed.

It is possible that there might be a secondary reason for the large locks that is not directly related to the size of vessels that would use the waterway. The considerable volume of water released at each lock would have had the effect of a flush on the river sections, such that it would have eased the passage over shallows. This might then have been a development of the 'flash lock', a devise used considerably on early river navigations. However, if the large locks were intended for the flush alone, then to continue with the same size along the still water canal to Kilkenny does not follow.

Across the river from Kilferagh, and just a little way downstream, are the remains of Dunbell Guard Lock. This was a single set of gates that acted as a flood lock for the long canal stretch beyond. Once again all the facing stones have been removed but the rubble backing of the abutments can still be seen. The 1½ mile of canal that follows is clearly visible, first as a clear-cut excavation in the grounds of Nore Cottage and then as a shallow depression through the fields. Unfortunately the sight of Dunbell Lock has been completely obliterated by recent gravel workings. The 1761 map shows a circular lock-house with a domed roof but like the other illustrations, it may have been a figment of the cartographer's imagination.

The Bennettsbridge canal begins at Kilree Lock. This was almost certainly a flood lock with a single set of gates. However its probable location was so heavily overgrown that a detailed inspection was impossible. On the approach to the bridge that crosses the river there is an arched bridge over a depression that follows the course of the canal. Although the Bennettsbridge canal was excavated, the lock by which it was to have entered the river at Maidenhall was never constructed. Some work may have been carried out in the years up to 1777 when desultory attempts were made to complete the navigation. Where Maidenhall Lock would have been there are some larger than usual stones incorporated into a farm wall and a visible depression may have been the start of excavations for the lock chamber.

A study of the 6in Ordnance Survey together with an inspection of selected sites, confirms suspicions that no works were executed below Maidenhall. It could be assumed that the navigation was begun at the wrong end. Had work started from the tidal river, trade could have begun on each length as it was completed. It was a mistake frequently made by early canal engineers. But the assumption is contrary to the fact that a canal and lock was constructed to bypass the rapids at Inistioge. The 1761 report records, "that at the town of Ennisteague, in the obediance of the Navigation Board in Dublin, to build a bridge and bay, there is a fine stone bridge 300 feet in length, nearly completed". The east arch of this bridge appears to have been the one intended for the canal. There is a depression in the meadow upstream from the arch, and downstream it continues as a water course until it joins the river at a point known as Lock Quay. There is a stone quay immediately downstream from where the canal enters the river, but nowhere can be found the remains of a lock. It is possible that it was a simple affair with only a single set of gates.

However, the enigma of the Inistioge canal, and indeed one of the puzzles right along the navigation, is that the bridge arches can only pass a maximum beam of eleven feet. In 1787 it was reported that the boats using the river to Thomastown were 52ft by 10ft 9in beam. But I wonder which came first, the boats or the bridge? The 1787 report was part of a plan put forward by William Chapman (an engineer with links to the Grand Canal, Shannon and Barrow Navigations) to continue the navigation from Bennettsbridge to Thomastown. He estimated that 14 locks would be needed and recommended that they be made 60ft by 11ft. Nothing came of the scheme but it seems likely that the river was used as a navigation of sorts up to Thomastown.

In addition to Chapman's 1787 scheme a number of other attempts were made to revive the Nore Navigation. Six years later Chapman produced a plan which included a branch to Goresbridge. In 1801 George Joyce proposed a completely new navigation from Esker, five miles above Kilkenny, to Inistioge. He also recommended a branch to connect to the Barrow. In 1911 the Shuttleworth Commission reconsidered the Nore Navigation, again with a view to an entirely new canal, but no action was taken.

Up until recent times sand barges worked on the tidal portion of the river and cargoes were delivered to the small quays upon its banks. Near a number of these quays stand the remains of lime kilns. The reach below Inistioge is dotted with islands and is of considerable charm. It is still possible to sail the river to Lock Quay....to the beginning of a baffling and enigmatic scheme to connect Kilkenny to the sea.

WATERFORD ESTUARY

Up until the mid1950's Grand Canal barges ran a weekly service from Dublin to Waterford. The journey took four days whereas our travels from Dublin to St Mullins had taken four months. But on the last leg to Waterford we equaled the speed of the barges. It is simply a matter of catching the tide.

On the morning of our departure high water was at eleven. To while the time away until then we took a final walk into the village. Not that St Mullins was all that dear to our hearts. It is a disappointment, a beauty spot gone wrong. What was once honest, simple and true is now an ostentatious show for the visitor: teas, ices, and minerals, plastic gnomes, toy-town fencing, and fussy flower beds. Many of the visitors come to see the monastery, the remains of which are topped by a 'No Dumping' sign. The best way to see St Mullins is to shot passed on the tide.

Below the lock the river begins to broaden out and Jessica surged forward at what seemed to be a terrific rate after weeks at a crawl. It is a passage of rare beauty. The Barrow has carved a course between the foothills of Brandon Hill and the Blackstairs Mountains. Steep wooded slopes and sheer cliffs rise from the waterside. It is a tantalizing journey for the tide hurries you on and there is no easy means of stopping to explore. Yet, as I know from a later visit, it is a locality well worth exploration. Five miles below St Mullins a stream joins the flow of the river and if you were to follow the footpath that runs beside it you would come to Pollmounty Mill. There has been a woolen mill at Pollmounty ever since the 17th century, and perhaps even before that. The mill is still working and its methods and machinery have not changed in the last hundred years.

By early afternoon we had reached New Ross and in order to meet the tide lower down we moored there for an hour or so. More recently, the town has developed into one of Ireland's gateways to Europe and it might now be difficult now to find a spare inch of quay to tie to. This is not the first time that the fortunes of New Ross have changed and the town busy with shipping. If you visit the Auctioneer's Office at the end of the quay you will see a photograph that dates from the last century. It shows the same quayside busy with barges and sailing schooners. The history of the Port of New Ross can be traced back to the Middle Ages. In 1265 no fewer than 600 seamen from the crews of the ships at anchor helped to build the walls of the town. I imagine that there has always been a tradition of ship building at New Ross and no doubt barges have been built there in the past. But it is unlikely that the ship builders of New Ross have ever had closer connections with the canals than they do today. At a yard below the quay they build huge box shaped craft and these are the floating units of the revolutionary 'Lighter Aboard Ship' scheme. The barges are towed in trains along the major inland waterways of the world and when loaded aboard their parent ship they carry their cargoes across oceans: in effect, floating shipping containers.

Just above New Ross the Barrow is joined by the Nore, and twelve miles beyond the town the combined rivers are met by the waters of the Suir. Together they form the Waterford Estuary. It is at Checkpoint that river becomes estuary and it was there that we anchored to wait for the incoming tide to carry us up to Waterford.

The City of Waterford stands on the south bank of the Suir six miles from Checkpoint. Like several other Irish seaports, it traces its origin to the Vikings, whose fleets appeared in the harbour in 914. The major feature of Waterford is its three-quarter mile quay. It is called successively; Merchant's Quay, Meagher's Quay, Coal Quay and Custom House Quay. The best small boat mooring is the floating jetty that lies off Merchant's Quay. It was during our stay there that we saw Ireland's last remaining commercial inland waterway traffic. Each day a barge with a cargo of grain came down from Carrick.

The barge unloaded at the quay across from us and at the first opportunity we rowed across to talk to her crew. There are two barges, both of them worked by the same crew. They take back the empty and immediately set off again with the full. It is a round trip of thirty miles, all of which is in tidal water. They carry a cargo of 70 tons. There used to be five boats running all the year round but now the traffic is only in the grain season. I asked them how many more years the service was likely to last. They answered, "Until she sinks".

Our original intention had been to sail Jessica home from Ireland, but by the time we were ready to leave autumn gales had begun to brood over the Irish Sea. We spent a fortnight waiting for settled conditions. It was difficult enough for us to tear ourselves away from a land that we had come to love so much and we had no wish to suffer a protracted farewell. As Diana said, waiting takes too long! Instead we negotiated Jessica's passage home aboard a ship that was sailing for Liverpool. Early one morning we watched her being hoisted aboard. We had no sooner followed her to England than we wished ourselves back again: back to the Grand Canal, the Shannon and the Barrow. It was a wish that we never imagined could come true. But in Ireland they have a saying that the inevitable never happens but the unexpected often does.

ACKNOWLEDGEMENTS

I thank all of those who shared their experiences and helped us on our way. Many are now in the next world but I feel sure that if there are canals and rivers their too, they will they will have the channel deep and the locks ready for our arrival.

Additionally, I thank my daughter Tania for her help in seeing this book through to print.

Made in the USA
Columbia, SC
08 April 2019